Library of Liberal Thought

Æsthetic
Benedetto Croce
with a new introduction by John McCormick

The Case for Modern Liberalism
Charles Frankel
with a new introduction by Thelma Z. Lavine

Changing Disciplines
John A. Ryle

Congressional Government
Woodrow Wilson
with a new introduction by William F. Connelly, Jr.

Constitutional Government in the United States
Woodrow Wilson
with a new introduction by Sidney A. Pearson, Jr.

The Correspondence of John Stuart Mill and Auguste Comte
Oscar A. Haac, editor

New Deal Days: 1933-1934
Eli Ginzberg

The New Democracy
Walter E. Weyl
with a new introduction by Sidney A. Pearson, Jr.

Party Government
E. E. Schattschneider
with a new introduction by Sidney A. Pearson, Jr.

Peace and War
Robert A. Rubinstein and Mary LeCron Foster, editors

Politics and Administration
Frank J. Goodnow
with a new introduction by John A. Rohr

Politics and Religious Consciousness in America
George Armstrong Kelly

Presidential Leadership
Pendleton Herring
with a new introduction by Sidney A. Pearson, Jr.

Quest for Equality in Freedom
Francis M. Wilhoit

Tocqueville and American Civilization
Max Lerner

Toward a New Enlightenment
Paul Kurtz

The Transatlantic Persuasion
Robert Kelley

The Political Relations
of Congress and the Chief Executive

Presidential
Leadership

Pendleton Herring

With a new introduction by Sidney A. Pearson, Jr.

Transaction Publishers
New Brunswick (U.S.A.) and London (U.K.)

Second printing 2009

New material this edition copyright © 2006 by Transaction Publishers, New Brunswick, New Jersey. Originally published in 1940 by Rinehart & Company, Inc.

This book is printed on acid-free paper that meets the American National Standard for Permanence of Paper for Printed Library Materials.

Library of Congress Catalog Number: 2005053819
ISBN: 978-1-4128-0556-8
Printed in the United States of America

Library of Congress Cataloging-in-Publication Data

Herring, Pendleton, 1903-
    Presidential leadership : the political relations of Congress and the chief executive / Pendleton Herring; with a new introduction by Sidney A. Pearson.
        p. cm.—(Library of liberal thought)
Originally published: New York : Rinehart & Co., 1940.
Includes bibliographical references and index.
ISBN 1-4128-0556-2 (pbk. : alk. paper)
    1. Executive power—United States. 2. United States—Politics and government. 3. United States. Congress—Powers and duties. I. Title. II. Series.

JK516.H4   2006
352.23'6'0973—dc22   2005053819

To my aunts

ANNETTE SHERWOOD and PEARL HERRING

In appreciation of their unfailing welcome in Washington

*And so it was, that as
oft as he passed by, he
turned in thither to eat
bread.*—II Kings 4:8.

Contents

Transaction Introduction: The Founders'
Presidency Meets the Modern World ... ix

Acknowledgments ... liii

Preface ... lv

I. The Political Basis of Presidential Power ... 1

II. Congressional Behavior ... 21

III. Methods of Presidential Control ... 46

IV. Proposals for Change ... 73

V. The President's Entourage ... 92

VI. The Limits of Presidential Responsibility ... 111

VII. The Strength of Presidential Leadership ... 128

Appendices:

I.   War Powers of the President   147

II.   Presidential Cabinets   164

Index   167

★ ★ ★ ★ ★ ★

Transaction Introduction

The Founders' Presidency Meets the Modern World*

O N THE FACE of it, Pendleton Herring's defense of the modern presidency in *Presidential Leadership* (1940) seems to trace its philosophical lineage back to the founding debates over the nature of the presidency. Alexander Hamilton in *The Federalist* described "energy" in the office of the president as the very heart of good government: "A feeble executive implies a feeble execution of the government. A feeble execution is but another phrase for a bad execution: and a government ill executed, whatever it may be in theory, must be, in practice, a bad government" (Fed. 70). It is perhaps the most oft-quoted passage ever penned on the presidency. But more importantly, it reflects one of the core ideas of Hamilton's contribution to the founders' "new science of politics": that the modern science of popular government, while not synonymous with executive power, was certainly compatible with it.[1] Indeed, in Hamilton's formulation,

* I would like to thank my friend and colleague Matt Franck for reading several drafts of this manuscript and making it better than it would otherwise be. The errors and shortcomings remain, of course, my own.

presidential leadership was to be the engine of the new government. It was and remains one of the central ideas in the American science of politics, but it is problematic in every respect.

On the one hand, arguments supporting strong presidential leadership based on constitutional design confront the obvious dilemma that the Constitution does not appear to have been assembled to facilitate executive leadership: The founders spoke of limited government with enumerated powers and not of presidential leadership. For the founders of all particular persuasions, presidential leadership was understood to be leadership within a written constitution. On the other hand, we are also familiar with the Anti-Federalist argument that the presidency represented monarchial tendencies and was therefore the enemy of republican government. This side of the founding debates has never entirely lost its appeal, a point Hamilton acknowledged both at the Constitutional Convention and in *The Federalist*.[2] The Anti-Federalist doubted that the Constitution would be adequate to contain executive leadership, especially in times of crisis. Herring's approach to understanding the problems and irony of presidential leadership in the American constitutional system should be read as one of the significant attempts to resolve the apparent tensions in the founders' conception of the office. The merits of his contribution will turn on whether or not his approach helps to deepen our understanding of this evident tension.

Hamilton's famous dictum on the presidency has always therefore presented a dilemma for students of American politics, a dilemma that lay at the heart of Herring's work. Most students of the presidency acknowledge that the overall constitutional design is not obviously intended to promote presidential leadership, however much Hamilton thought it essential for effective republican government and however much Herring sought to reassure his readers that an energetic president was safe for democracy. Advocates of the president as the engine of American government have had to contend with Madison's observation, also in *The Federalist*: "In republican government, the legislative authority necessarily predominates" (Fed. 51). Madison's point, while it certainly does not contradict Hamilton's dictum, reminds us that the president, strong or weak, must expect to meet with powerful opposition from the legislature that is built into the constitutional design. The full implications of presidential leadership, especially in crisis times, will always depend at least as much on time, place, and circumstance as constitutional design. After the ratification of the Constitution, an energetic president versus legislative dominance quickly became the heart of the philosophical quarrel that developed between Hamilton on the one side and Madison and Jefferson on the other side during the 1790s.

What is significant about this original quarrel is that both Hamilton and Jefferson-Madison grounded their arguments in conflicting constitutional interpretations, both of which were plausible readings of constitutional intent in a legal sense. The heart of the issue Herring confronted is whether the founders' new science of politics, built around a separation of powers and with a long tradition of legislative dominance, is adequate to support energetic presidential leadership, most especially in times of crisis—when executive leadership may be essential for the survival, not to mention the general well being, of the regime. Does the analysis of leadership in such times require the abandonment of a legalistic reading of the Constitution? If so, what form should such abandonment take? What happens to the constitutional basis of American democracy if a particular crisis raises regime-level questions, such as Civil War or the Great Depression of the 1930s, that seem to call for a response that is beyond the scope of the ordinary constitutional structure of American politics?

Herring's approach was grounded in a traditional form of institutional analysis but, unlike the founding quarrel, it was not based
on a legalistic reading of the Constitution. Instead, his defense
of a strong president was built on the assumption that presidential leadership could be understood apart from philosophical dis-
putes of the sort that raged during the founding era. Leadership
was rooted in the personal qualities of the president and in the
nature of the particular crisis confronted either successfully or
unsuccessfully. It is an approach with both strengths and weaknesses that need to be better understood because Herring's pioneering approach has been the dominant approach to presidential
studies since he helped to introduce it. It has rightly been labeled
the "behavioral persuasion" in political science.[3]

Reading both of these statements by Hamilton and Madison
from *The Federalist* in tandem has led many students of the
presidency to see presidential leadership as **the** great desideratum
of American constitutional government.[4] Is it possible to support both energy in the presidency *and* the Constitution simultaneously? Or is *The Federalist* simply incoherent as a science of
politics, at least on this point? Most of the nineteenth-century
constitutional theory and practice seemed to belong to Madison
and Jefferson's restricted view of presidential power. Even
Lincoln's exercise of executive power during the Civil War appeared to many at the time and immediately after the war to be
a temporary and unique exception to the Jeffersonian view of
limited executive power. But beginning with the Progressive Era
in the late nineteenth century, there has been a marked tendency
among scholars to side with Hamilton in the sense that an energetic presidency is, or ought to be, the locus of modern democracy. It was in the political science of the Progressive Era that
the separation of powers came to be seen as an obstacle to democratic government, which was increasingly defined in terms of

executive dominance in policymaking. Far from an arrangement designed to preserve democracy, the separation of powers came to be seen as an arrangement designed to thwart democracy.

It was during the Progressive Era that academic debates over the separation of powers significantly shifted the terms of debates over executive power and, with it, the very idea of presidential leadership. Many Progressives looked to public opinion rather than the Constitution as a source of energy in the executive. Furthermore, they tended to see public opinion as something that operated outside the Constitution and energized the executive beyond any formal powers that might be derived from the Constitution. It is on this point that the Progressive tradition broke with the founders' science of politics. Energy in the executive was seen by Progressives as something independent of constitutional form and structure and even hostile to the very form of the founders' Constitution. When Progressives such as Woodrow Wilson or Herbert Croly defended Hamilton's view of the presidency, it was therefore something of a Trojan horse argument. A powerful executive was to be grafted onto the Constitution based on principles foreign to it. The debate came to a head during the administration of Franklin Roosevelt when the New Deal provoked a constitutional crisis over presidential power. It was widely acknowledged that the economic crisis of the Great Depression required the exercise of presidential leadership to a degree perhaps unprecedented since Lincoln. But the very exercise of such power seemed to expose a rift between the theory and practice of American government—a rift that harkened back to Hamilton versus Madison-Jefferson. Could it be that the Constitution would have to be ignored or at least suspended in times of extraordinary crisis in order to sustain a democratic regime? Or could sufficient energy in the executive be found and sustained in a way that would not wreck the Constitution?

The place of executive leadership in a constitutional system seemingly designed for legislative dominance has increasingly divided students of American government into opposing schools of thought on the political science of the founding. How sides are chosen on the basis of presidential leadership then lies at the bottom of most systemic reform proposals in American politics. And while the nature of the debate probably admits of no definitive argument that silences all others, Pendleton Herring's 1940 study of energy in the presidency of Franklin Roosevelt, *Presidential Leadership*, should be read as one of the significant contributions to this ongoing argument over regime principles. In it he makes the case that an energetic president is not a threat to democratic government "rightly understood." But the phrase "rightly understood" masks a subtle and significant point of departure in how academic political science has come to understand American government. It is a departure from the political science of both Hamilton and Madison-Jefferson that at the same time abandons some of the conspicuous features of the Progressive tradition. It is a departure sharpened by the characteristic thought of the Progressive Era. And it is both the difference and the similarities with the Wilsonian tradition that make *Presidential Leadership* the pioneering landmark in presidential studies that it is.

Political Science, Presidential Leadership and Progressive Politics

Trying to understand executive leadership solely as a matter of theory, and relying solely on *The Federalist* as a source of philosophical light, have led many subsequent observers to view presidential leadership as the Achilles heel of American democracy. The United States seems to have been fortunate that during times of national peril, such as the Civil War or the Great Depression, the nation found a leader who was up to the task. But as Madison also noted, we cannot expect that enlightened leaders will always be at the helm, and a well-founded government must recognize this fact of political life. Read as a legal treatise, *The Federalist* is frustratingly ambiguous regarding the nature and sources of presidential leadership. When the founders thought of "proper" presidential leadership under the Constitution they most commonly thought of George Washington, and they worried considerably over executive prerogative powers that had been cast in such stark relief by Locke. Machiavelli's prince was an example to be avoided and not to be emulated.[5] But Washington was thought of in terms of character, and they well understood that to a very large degree the person would make the office.

Progressive scholars such as Woodrow Wilson winced at James Bryce's suggestion that "great men" are never chosen president in the United States, but were half afraid that he might be right.[6] What seems to be required, especially in crisis times, is a charismatic model of presidential leadership, unshackled by institutional restraints, in order to make the system, or whatever may be left of it after such radical tinkering, work. It is a view of democratic government very much at odds with the founders' problem of "taming the prince" by a series of checks and balances.[7] This is particularly true in the liberal-progressive scholarship that developed to explain and analyze American democratic theory prior to and immediately after World War I, the era of scholarship in which Herrington's work appeared and took shape.

The notion that the political science of *The Federalist* was incoherent on the face of it first occurred to Woodrow Wilson when he was an undergraduate at Princeton in the 1870s. Later, as a graduate student at Johns Hopkins, he saw a weak presidency as the fatal flaw of the American constitutional system. When he later seemed to promote a strong presidency in *Constitutional Government* (1908), it was premised on a radically new model of executive power that had little in common with either Hamilton or Madison. It was a new model presidency built on a rhetorical leadership of public opinion that would overwhelm institutional barriers designed to prevent such a concentration of power.[8] He did not so much attack the separation of powers in his later work, as he had done earlier, as he mostly ignored it in his new model presidency. This new model presidency of Wilson's was to be linked to public opinion by responsible political parties along the lines of a parliamentary system. And it was this model that shaped Herring's work. There was a widespread sense among scholars in the Wilsonian mold, such as Herbert Croly for example, that Hamilton's support for a strong executive represented a theoretical understanding of how government ought to work, whereas Madison's constitutional design, most especially in his defense of the separation of powers, appeared to be a practical block to Hamilton's idea of the presidency and it was a far more accurate model of how the system worked in practice.[9] Particularly in the case of an increasingly complex bureaucracy, it seemed as if presidents had no real control over the direction of administration, which in turn meant the direction of national policy.[10] The Progressive view of administration as a pyramid with the president at the apex of the pyramid was one of the conspicuous features of early work on public administration.[11] In any case, one of the hallmarks of the Progressives' attack on the founders' Constitution was their identification of the presidency as the locus of democratic government and they were less interested in "taming the prince" than in letting him out of his constitutional cage.

A presidency hobbled by the separation of powers seemed to open a rift between Hamilton and Madison that made *The Federalist* an unlikely source of inspiration for any science of politics, especially in the Progressive tradition that made the translation of majority will into effective public policy the basis of its claim to be a political science founded on democratic principles.[12] The common denominator among otherwise different scholars in this tradition has been that they have generally sided with Hamilton against Madison, albeit with some qualifications. Hamilton's defense of executive prerogative was widely viewed as still too much constrained by constitutional interpretation, but at least he understood the importance of executive power better than the Jeffersonians. In practical terms, the newly minted liberal-progressive political science meant hostility to what was perceived as the theoretical incoherence of *The Federalist*. Academic political science, insofar as it followed the Wilsonian model, was premised on the need for a "new" new science of politics that put an institutionally unfettered presidency at the heart of democratic theory as it elevated the importance of presidential personality. Herbert Croly, for one, candidly acknowledged that this meant a transformation of the American understanding of democratic government in all of its essentials, including even a new Declaration of Independence freed from its natural rights logic.[13]

The liberal-progressive reformers who followed Wilson's lead made it an article of faith that the English parliamentary system of democratic government was superior to the American form of democracy for any number of reasons, but preeminent among them was the concentration of executive power in the prime minister. The concentration of executive power was typically viewed as a prerequisite for responsible party government in a democratic mold, and was the basis for their routine critique of the separation of powers. Prior to the administration of Franklin Roosevelt in 1933, it was not at all clear to these students of American politics that the Constitution could provide an adequate framework for the sort of presidential leadership that seemed necessary to lead the country in crisis times. Lincoln was an exception, and Wilson's own inability to secure the League of Nations in the Senate seemed to confirm the liberal-progressive thesis. And they certainly read the Great Depression beginning in 1929 as the greatest domestic crisis since the Civil War. Further, their academic dominance typically meant that the founders' science of politics was filtered through a Wilsonian interpretation of the ends of governance in general: that the final purpose of government was to make policy in accord with an enlightened public opinion. The disappearance of the idea of limited government with enumerated powers could not help but have far-reaching consequences for how the office of the president was understood.

More tradition-minded critics of the Wilsonian view argued that his new model presidency was a prescription for constitutional dictatorship and that the concentration of power to the degree that Wilson and the Progressives advocated was a threat to democratic government. For example, President Taft's defense of executive leadership rooted in constitutional prerogative powers in his famous quarrel with his predecessor, Teddy Roosevelt, reflected at least part of this critique of the liberal-progressive argument.[14] But Taft's view of presidential prerogative powers was still rooted in the founding, and his reference points were the republican principles of the founding debates. In this sense, Taft seemed to represent the past of theoretical debates over executive leadership rather than the future. The emerging liberal-progressive science of politics may have commanded the allegiance of many academic scholars, but the Jeffersonian tradition of limited government articulated by Taft and others still carried considerable appeal among the public and had a respectable following among some scholars. Herring's *Presidential Leadership* was written as a response to both of these schools—the two sides of the founding and the Wilsonian Progressives. In it he staked out a perspective that borrowed from each but was not exclusively rooted in either of them.

Herring did not advance an entirely Wilsonian response to either Hamilton or Jefferson on presidential leadership, however much certain aspects of the liberal-progressive argument may have influenced him. First of all, his own work in the study of administration told him that administration in the federal government was scarcely a pyramid with the president perched at the apex. And it further taught him that this was not such a bad thing for a democratic government. Instead, his thesis was part of an emerging behavioral interpretation of American politics that accepted the existing constitutional design as "given" and tried to show how it did and could be made to work without radical redesign. Even in heroic times, presidential leadership did not necessarily require a heroic president so much as it required a mastery of administration, a point Herring stressed earlier in his *Public Administration and the Public Interest* (1936).[15] Presidential leadership in Herring's treatise is more akin to a political craftsman's attention to the details of his trade. Administration and policymaking were part of the "given" of American democracy and Herring was concerned with how to make them efficient, very much in an economic sense, rather than questioning their desirability. The presidency of Franklin Roosevelt was his model, but his analysis did not yield the heroic conception of the office that has dominated so many scholars looking back on the New Deal. In addition, Herring never saw any reason to change the form of American democracy to a parliamentary model, and as a consequence helps to restore some attention to matters of form, such as the separation of powers. The founders' system was sufficiently plastic to be able to cope with even the most extreme crisis.

The first hundred days of the administration of Franklin Roosevelt made it clear to Herring that the Madison-Jefferson view of limited government was not adequate in times of national crisis. And at the same time, the founders' new science of politics was largely irrelevant to both explain and analyze Roosevelt and the New Deal. Pendleton Herring's *Presidential Leadership* explained both why and how Roosevelt's leadership marked a defining moment in the development of academic understanding of the nature of American democracy, independent of the founders' science of politics. It remains one of the best analytic studies of how Roosevelt was able to implement the New Deal in the context of a constitutional system that many in the liberal-progressive tradition had all but given up on. As such, Herring's work deserves a close analysis both for the historical light it sheds on Roosevelt and for the subsequent development of presidential scholarship. Presidential leadership requires opportunities, which a crisis may provide, but it also requires a person who can take advantage of those opportunities and use them to the common good. Both Herbert Hoover and Franklin Roosevelt confronted the Great Depression, but whereas the former was confounded by the problem and left office a failure, the latter embraced it and died in office widely regarded as one of our greatest presidents. *Presidential Leadership* is a pioneer study of the American presidency during this critical moment, a study in the then emerging behavioral school of academic political science. It should be seen as the prototype for works such as Richard Neustadt's *Presidential Power* that followed and were very much in the tradition of Herring.

Pendleton Herring and the Politics of Democracy

When Pendleton Herring was elected president of the American Political Science Association in 1953 the event signaled the growing movement toward behavioralism in the social sciences generally and political science in particular. Herring was the choice of those scholars in academic political science who had first organized the Committee on Political Behavior in 1949 and who were most influential in establishing survey research and quantitative theory as the theoretical heart of academic political science.[16] In Herring's understanding, behavioralism meant the modernization of the study of politics, a modernization that meant a relegation of traditional, normative theory to the realm of abstraction.[17] He did not engage the founders' science of politics so much as he chose to ignore it whenever possible and sought instead to forge a newer political science that was less encumbered with what he thought of as "normative" concerns. Political science, properly understood, was about the observation of specific political behavior in fact and not very much concerned about how things ought to be in an abstract sense. At one level, this meant a critique of much of the Progressive Era scholarship because it had spent too much time speculating on how to change the constitutional system rather than observing how it actually operated. The Progressive error was to spend too much time disputing with the founders at the philosophical level and as a consequence neglecting the more empirical study of how American government and politics actually operate. Herring believed the constitutional system could be made to work better than the Progressives typically thought, but before it could be made to work, more analytic effort would be required to understand how it worked in practice. Theory largely meant observing practice and then linking it to performance, often and typically defined as the translation of public opinion into policy.[18] Such was the promise of behavioralism in political science.

In his inaugural address as president of the APSA, he said, "I think that most of us see with clarity today that our political problems are not to be disposed of by miracles of leadership.... To suggest, as some do, that our governmental craft should be exchanged for an improved model more responsive to the helm is beside the point. Our hope must lie in better seamanship."[19] At first glance it might seem odd that such a close student of American politics would write on "presidential leadership" and shortly thereafter reject what he calls "the miracle of leadership." Yet the contradiction is more apparent than real. In contrast with much of the scholarship of the Progressive Era, Herring accepted as "given" the existing institutional structure of American politics. The president was one actor, among others, who operated within a system of institutional "givens" and was not the sole person who drove a political agenda. In his best-known work, *The Politics of Democracy: American Parties in Action* (1940), he made the case for decentralized American parties against the "responsible party" school of disciplined parties associated with Woodrow Wilson.[20] He was also critical of what might be called the "heroic school" of presidential leadership, that is, the notion that the presidency is the center of the constitutional system and requires leadership of outsized proportions to steer the ship of state.[21] Each of these points helped to set him apart from other advocates of the Progressive view of American government. Leadership required political skills and could not be divorced from the mundane business of legislative, party, and public opinion coalition building. And *Presidential Leadership* is a chronicle of precisely how Roosevelt used his political skills to achieve what he wanted without a heroic vision in either the founding or liberal-progressive sense of the term.

In Herring's account energy in the executive boils down to the political skill of the executive in dealing with Congress more than any other single factor. In Herring's account, Roosevelt was able to lead the country through the darkest days of the Great Depression not merely because the crisis lent itself to the concentration of political power in the president, which is true enough but insufficient as an explanation of why Roosevelt ranks as one of our great presidents. Roosevelt achieved greatness because he knew and understood the larger political and institutional context in which he operated and was able to use his own innate virtues to make the system work for the common good even though Herring seems to have regarded the very idea of the common good as problematic. To use Herring's metaphor, Roosevelt was a great president because he knew both how to steer the ship of state and the mechanics of how the ship actually worked below deck. Knowledge of one, to the exclusion of the other, would have dramatically reduced Roosevelt from a great president to a leader of somewhat lesser rank. Roosevelt's own inner drive was the indispensable ingredient that gave energy to his administration, but he still had to negotiate his way through a very much fragmented political system. The crisis did not concentrate power so much as it created an opportunity for Roosevelt to temporarily take maximum advantage of an inchoate public opinion and use it to his advantage.

We should note here that Herring's thinking about the presidency and presidential leadership shows considerable evolution from the first days of the New Deal until the eve of World War II. Herring was a junior professor at Harvard when Roosevelt was first elected in 1932. At the very outset of Roosevelt's administration he wrote a series of brief but sharp analytic descriptions for the *American Political Science Review* for what seemed to be a political revolution in Washington. They quickly established Herring as one of the most astute observers of American politics. One of his first observations was of the breakdown of the formal idea of the separation of powers in the crisis.[22] Surveying what has come to be known as the "first hundred days" of the Roosevelt administration, he noted, "Many so-called 'essential forms' became essentially empty formalities. The President had become a prime minister."[23] The reference to the president as a "prime minister" is a telling remark. It would appear that the Progressive idea of executive leadership in the parliamentary model had been realized without altering the form of government. But if Roosevelt could function for all practical purposes as a prime minister within the existing Constitution and without changing the Constitution, the situation called for a serious rethinking of the problem of presidential leadership. It was clear to Herring that the founding debates did not shed very much light on the subject.

What most struck Herring at the end of the first year of Roosevelt's administration was less what to make of the executive than whether Congress was a viable political institution: He rediscovered the wisdom of Madison that a viable Congress was a prerequisite for a viable presidency. Absent a responsible Congress, he asked, "Was the presidential system as such competent or even capable of meeting its responsibilities?"[24] If the president was to make the system work, he had to guard against an erosion of support in Congress. This meant that the separation of powers had to be defended, if only obliquely. "The paradox of the present system," he wrote, "is that only a conciliatory presidential policy can get the conflicting congressional *blocs* to work together—but then to what end?"[25] Coalition building was indeed a messy business that, in practice, seemed to offer little philosophical coherence in terms of policy. While the normative desirability of policy coherence led him in the direction of executive dominance in policy formulation, the reality of legislative power led him to conclude, "[T]he representative principle could not be maintained if confusion was to be avoided."[26] The system was not philosophically tidy and the crisis was breaking the mold of constitutional interpretation for both the founders and the Progressives. The result was that Herring could find little philosophical coherence in Roosevelt's New Deal agenda and little in the founding debates that could explain what was happening. The end of the first year "was one of compromise and concession directed toward curbing the more extreme demands of regions and classes... The President had shown himself to be an astute politician rather than a crusader."[27] Overall, the system demonstrated how weak are the devices for responsible leadership and control when strained by the forces of organized minorities. Indeed, "The 15,000 pages of the *Congressional Record* which set out the details [of the law-making process] add poignancy to the motto, 'In God We Trust.'"[28] If a heroic president was necessary to make the system work, and if Roosevelt was not a heroic president, what are we to make of the very idea of presidential leadership? And if traditional philosophic analysis does not adequately explain presidential leadership, what does?

Making Democracy Safe for the Modern Presidency

At the heart of Herring's approach to presidential leadership is the idea that the president can safely be entrusted with a concentration of power in times of crisis: not because of the virtue of the president or the virtue of the people, although Herring thinks both are in reasonably ample supply, but because of the way the government works in practice. The behavioral study of Roosevelt's New Deal suggested to Herring that the ends of liberal-progressive policymaking could be achieved without changing basic constitutional architecture. Woodrow Wilson had hinted at this in his last work, *Constitutional Government*, where he moved toward a theory of the presidency that argued the irrelevance of the separation of powers in theory. But Wilson had tied that movement to a constitutional theory that made the Constitution largely irrelevant. Herring was much more favorably disposed toward the utility of the existing institutions than was Wilson, but he was no less skeptical of the founders' legalistic conception of presidential power. A careful analysis of the facts, he thought, would strip away ideological presuppositions and force scholars to draw conclusions that flowed directly from the facts. It is this quality of honest and scrupulous attention to the facts of presidential politics in the formative period of the New Deal that give his work a lasting interest.

We look to executive leadership, as Herring notes in his Preface, "yet we face new tasks with old political equipment." The founders' Constitution, he thought, was not designed for the complex challenges of the modern world. His reading of how the system actually operates produced a sort of ambivalence in Herring's reflections on the separation of powers. On the one hand, the separation of powers is part of what he called the "folkways" of American politics. To that extent he agreed with the Wilsonian critique of the founders' Constitution. But on the other hand, he thought of behavioralism as "practical" in the sense that it could dispense with the endless and endlessly inconclusive arguments over the best form of popular government. "The practical question is how to work through or around such assumptions, for this is no time to overhaul our political structure."[29] The immediate problem was to meet the challenges of totalitarianism without losing the rule of law and the democratic character of the only polity we have. That meant presidential leadership within a system not designed for what he called "the complex necessities" of the modern world. Quoting Roosevelt, Herring approvingly observed, "Our Constitution is so simple and practical that it is always possible to meet extraordinary needs by changes in emphasis and arrangements without loss of essential form."[30] In other words, arguments over the form of government, which had so animated political debate in America from the founders through the Progressives, were largely irrelevant for either the theory or practice of American democracy.

Herring began his analysis of presidential leadership with a discussion of what he describes as "the political basis of presidential power." This is in sharp contrast with the founding arguments that presidential power was rooted in the Constitution, or even prerogative powers in the sense in which Locke used the term. The written Constitution was at the heart of Taft's quarrel with Roosevelt and the Progressives and it is what separated Herring from his predecessors in each camp. Herring insisted that before the president can be a leader of symbolic national purpose we must recognize that he must first be a politician who gets elected to the office. Whether or not he is later elevated to the status of heroic "statesman" will depend on historians more than voters. "The people elect the president, but they are not organized to support him in office: it is to Congress that he must constantly turn for the fulfillment of his objectives."[31] It was similar to the thesis later made famous by Richard Neustadt that presidential power is the "power to persuade."[32] Herring described the presidency as "a position of great power but [we] have made the full realization of that power dependent upon influence rather than legal authority."[33] It was a bold thesis at the time, developed with both subtlety and an impressive practical knowledge of how Roosevelt's New Deal actually operated during its first two terms. Furthermore, its subtlety helped to mask its break with the focus of much of the scholarship in the Progressive tradition.

Herring, very much following in Hamilton's footsteps on this point, denied that merely because the founders had conceived the office of the president to be above party conflict they also intended to create an ineffective office. Indeed, he noted that the founders also thought that in most instances the president would likely be elected by the legislative branch because the Electoral College would not reach a majority vote for president, "and the existence of this process would mean a direct connection between him and the power electing him and enacting his program."[34] The precise historical accuracy of Herring's point need not be discussed here. What is critical, however, is his recognition that a strong legislative role for the president is by no means precluded by constitutional design. He further denied, contra Woodrow Wilson, that they were inviting constant stalemate "when they subscribed to the Whig principle of checks and balances."[35] The separation of powers is an "anachronism" in Herring's opinion, but by itself it does not prohibit effective presidential leadership. It merely shifts the focus of leadership away from the legal concept of prerogative and toward the more personal basis of political persuasion. What upset the founders' calculations, in Herring's analysis, were the advent of political parties and the popular selection of the president that eventually took the legislature out of the political mix of selection. And there is no prospect for returning either to the original theoretical understanding of how the presidency is supposed to work or rewriting the Constitution in order to make the practice fit the liberal-progressive theory. The only alternative is to make presidential leadership work in the present context and without very much theoretical guidance from the past. It was at this point that behavioral research seemed to point to a way out of the theoretical impasse that had been reached in presidential studies. The emerging study of political behavior thus began to develop a theory of politics that was not immediately associated with preexisting schools of political science.[36]

Herring did agree with Wilson that the presidency has been one thing at one time and something else at another time due to the force of personality. "Observation discloses a succession of Congressional sessions and chief executives different in personal characteristics and in surrounding circumstances."[37] The problem of understanding the presidency arises when different writers begin to try to understand the office in formalized theoretical terms. This is not because the founders, for example, were necessarily right or wrong in their approach to presidential power, but because later conceptions that are typically at variance with the founders attempt to isolate a single factor in presidential leadership that the founders did not embrace and then critique them on that accord: It "is to impose an *a priori* frame of reference." It is to substitute argument for observation when the "uniformity of behavior...is clear and sufficient in itself."[38]

"Leadership in the making of public policy is fixed neither in the president nor in Congress," Herring observes.[39] And this is not a bad thing, but has its own political merit. There is a kind of cyclical operation to the separation of powers that alternates the power to make policy between the president and Congress. Unlike a parliamentary system, in which full responsibility for the policymaking process is focused on the exercise of executive power, the American system forces Congress to shoulder its share of political responsibility. The president does not represent the "general interest" in opposition to the special interests of Congress, but rather represents some special interests at the expense of others. "The president may serve as a leader-symbol to some people; to others he is simply one way to get things done."[40] This seems to be the very essence of the modern presidency defined in terms of political behavior to the virtual exclusion of individual motivation or philosophical principles. Whenever any one faction becomes permanently entrenched in a single branch of government, Congress or the presidency, "the whole system is endangered." What the separation of powers enables is a means to unblock the policy logjam by giving factions a way around dominance by a single institution. Beyond that, there is not very much to be said about it in theoretical terms. Consensus requires that compromise take place in the legislature as well as the executive branch, but that is a common feature of all healthy democracies.[41] The separation of powers creates rivalries for public support that have been one of the hallmarks of the American system. And consensus and compromise are at the heart of Herring's understanding of democracy.

In times of crisis the chief executive is the most effective rallying point for leadership, but authority is distributed between other institutions that make it virtually impossible for the president to sustain organized support. "Men are ruled by habit and directed by self-interest," and the habits engendered by the founders are too strong to be overcome by abstract philosophical argument even as the rationale for those arguments has faded with time. Fortunately, Herring thinks, it is not necessary to restructure the powers of government as suggested by the Progressives: "In time of crisis our government has ample powers; all governments must, indeed, possess them, if they would survive. But, if emergency means an increase in executive powers, the return to normal conditions is vastly facilitated by a reassertion of Congressional independence." Demobilization of the nation, after the crisis is past, will routinely be followed by a reassertion of the power of Congress. A particular crisis creates no necessary precedents that can be used to guide subsequent presidents facing a new crisis. The practical political consequence of this arrangement is that power can be concentrated in the president for the duration of a particular crisis with safety because it is unlikely to become a permanent part of the polity. The practical flexibility of the system is what ensures both long-term stability and the rule of law over the rule of men. Presidential power is contingent upon popular support. "There is nothing 'undemocratic' about such executive power. Fascism looms only when the opposition is no longer admitted as legitimate."[42] And whatever else may be said about the nature of the American regime, fascism does not seem to be an imminent threat despite the existence of certain fringe groups that might want to push politics in that direction.

The Place of Congress and Political Parties

Because effective presidential leadership depends upon an effective Congress, a question logically arises at this point: How effective is Congress in supporting a concentration of power in the executive? And if modern political parties are the link between a democratic culture and a popular form of government, how efficient is this arrangement for translating the popular will into effective and efficient government? The short answer to both questions is "not very," but behind that short answer is a more complex answer reflective of the behavioral approach to politics. It begins, as already noted, with a critique of the founders' constitutional design that is reminiscent of the Progressive critique associated with Wilson. But Herring rejects the philosophic call to reform the system along parliamentary lines and calls instead for a greater understanding of how the system actually works—warts and all. In a sense, Herring rejected the traditional Progressive call for parliamentary government as a way to concentrate executive power because Roosevelt's first hundred days showed how power could be concentrated without changing the constitutional form of American government. He acted as a prime minister would have acted, but without the intervening step of actually changing the Constitution. Further debates about the separation of powers seemed therefore to lose their urgency in American political science.

"Our national legislative assembly is still a continental Congress," Herring asserts. This observation was not intended as a compliment to either the patriotism or the political science of the founders. "While the presidential office has provided the most effective focal point for national policy within our system, it would be a vast oversimplification to assume that by virtue of his *influence* the president also has *control* as well.... Our legislative system tends to play into the hands of lobbyists. Professional manipulators can exploit the intricacy of the lawmaking process to forward their own ends."[43] Watching Congress work and rework the president's legislative agenda is much like watching sausage being made—the end product probably tastes better than the production of it warrants. But while this is less than the tidy argument of policy-government in the Wilsonian tradition of liberal-progressive political science, it does have its merits. "Wilson did less to influence Congress than either of his two predecessors.... He seemed to feel that he had expressed his opinion and there was no further argument."[44] If he had been less of an intellectual and more of a practical politician, such as FDR, he might have accomplished more. What the constitutional system requires to make it work are not intellectuals, but hard-working, practical politicians who later, after they are dead, may be referred to as "statesmen." In the halls of Congress, he wrote, "Congressmen remain untouched by what they regard as academic discussion."[45]

While the common good is seldom articulated and typically ignored through this process, Herring does note that "[t]he parties at interest do not feel required to talk to the galleries: they can talk to the point. To this extent the 'public interest' may be better served."[46] It is often overlooked in the policymaking process that a transfer of power from the legislative to the executive branch does not eliminate special interests; it only forces them to seek new and different channels of influence. And while responsibility is difficult to fix in this system because of institutional overlap in policymaking, it does tend to deflect full responsibility away from the president, unlike parliamentary systems where the executive has sole responsibility. This absence of sole responsibility in the executive can give him additional political flexibility.[47] And this, after all, was one of the ends of the Wilsonian school of presidential leadership. It does mean, however, that effective presidential leadership will depend far more than Progressives realized on an effective organization of Congress.

The problem of congressional organization is rooted in its principle of local representation. The Progressives in the responsible party school required, among other things, that parties represent a national interest and not merely an aggregate of local interests.[48] But one of Herring's points in *Presidential Leadership* is that the very absence of disciplined parties helps to fix responsible presidential leadership. Practical presidential responsibility was exercised primarily through a series of parliamentary tricks and maneuvers that were directed at the president's own party as much as the opposition. But while it was economically inefficient in the sense that billions of dollars were wasted or misspent on local pork-barrel projects, it was politically efficient in the sense that it helped to cement broad-based political consensus. It was a reminder that political efficiency is not synonymous with economic efficiency.

If Congress were better organized, Herring says, we might hear less about the need for a concentration of executive power. But a fragmented Congress reflects the fragmented nature of public opinion. Democratic Party control of both houses of Congress was essential to the passage of New Deal legislation during the first hundred days of Roosevelt's administration, but it was not sufficient.[49] "Party responsibility can only be erected on a strong national party organization that actively aids in local elections. The presidential policies of the New Deal, we are now discovering, never permeated the Democratic party as a whole."[50] Congress is a place of "guerrilla warfare" where both parties are often divided against themselves as well as against each other and the president, regardless of party. Local and sectional interests are dominant in a system characterized by loose party discipline. But unlike the Wilsonian Progressives, Herring reaffirmed throughout his career the idea that "our traditional party system continues to fulfill the vital need for compromise, for consensus seeking, for finding the terms upon which government by consent can go forward."[51] The separation of powers forces government to operate on a consensus rather than simple majority rule.[52] Far from being a weakness, however, it can be a source of strength. And in times of emergency Congress is capable of swift action. It is not entirely a sausage factory: "Congress has also exhibited nobler traits when occasions demand."[53] And there is no greater occasion than war when such traits are most in demand. It is the ultimate test of the flexibility of the system to respond to presidential leadership.

War as the Molder of the Constitution

When *Presidential Leadership* appeared in 1940, the question on almost everyone's mind was the war in Asia and Europe and whether or not the United States could avoid it. And as Hamilton had pointedly noted in *The Federalist*, "It is of the nature of war to increase the executive at the expense of the legislative authority." (Fed. 8) A war was bound to increase executive power at a time when Herring was trying to show that such an increase during the New Deal did not in fact upset democratic government. The focus of Herring's *APSR* articles was how Roosevelt was able to implement his domestic agenda. War seemed more distant, or at least more abstract. But by 1940 it was clear that domestic politics had been largely replaced by problems of foreign affairs—specifically fascism and the twin threats of war in Europe and the Pacific. Herring alludes to fascism and its conflict with democracy frequently, and it is never far from his mind in every phase of discussing presidential leadership. His extensive inclusion of relevant war statutes at the end of his work shows just how much it was on his mind.

As a practical matter, much of the domestic opposition to the concentration of presidential power might in the future turn on war powers, and Herring's behavioral analysis of presidential leadership had to bear the weight of imminent war. Most especially in this context, he was acutely aware that the opposition to formal American entanglement in foreign affairs had a pedigree that stretched back beyond the Progressive Era and to the founders. On this score it was the founding arguments and not merely modern academic scholarship that would have to be answered. It is therefore essential to any assessment of Herring's influence on presidential studies that we compare his work, at least briefly, with what he took to be his competition—the founders and the Progressives.

At first glance, the practical question raised by Herring's approach to presidential leadership is whether lessons learned in the context of domestic policy could somehow be applied to problems of war and peace in foreign policy. Is the problem of war and peace for any regime, but especially a popular regime such as the United States, so qualitatively different that the rules of the one sphere of action are inapplicable in the other? Herring thought that the rules governing the two areas of executive policymaking were essentially the same. And therein lays the basic strength of his work as well as its limitations. Can presidential leadership be compartmentalized this way? Are there "two presidencies," as some have argued, with one source of presidential power for domestic affairs and a second source of power for foreign affairs?[54] Or is the source of power the same in each case as Herring states, in the personal political qualities of the man who occupies the office? "Presidential power depends upon the incumbent's personal influence and upon his manipulative ability plus his capacity to judge the currents of his time and direct these forces into constructive lines. Presidential leadership seems to rest upon a personal rather than a partisan basis."[55] If the source is the same, as Herring suggests, can the philosophical basis of the founders' science of political science be ignored to the degree Herring's approach demands? If presidential power is different in the two areas, are the qualities of leadership required in each area analogous, or are they different? There is a compelling case to be made that the founders, across a wide spectrum of opinion with regard domestic matters, tended to see the president as preeminent in war and foreign affairs.[56] The Madison-Jeffersonian case for legislative supremacy did not apply to foreign affairs. If Herring's approach had not so studiously avoided constitutional analysis he might have found a way to bridge this conceptual divide that has so perplexed American political science.

Herring is more circumspect in his discussion of presidential war powers than his discussion of domestic powers, but the general thrust of his argument seems obvious enough. The exercise of war powers requires prudential judgment, and Herring's emphasis on political behavior was intended to highlight the practical judgment of political leaders. As he had analyzed the domestic agenda of the New Deal, he saw no challenge to regime principles in the temporary concentration of power in the president, and there was no reason to believe the concentration of war powers in the president would prove an exception. He includes in his appendices a series of documents that codify general and presidential war powers within the rule of law. It points toward a very legalistic reasoning and as such one that seems oddly out of place in the context of his broader reading of the place of the Constitution and how it does, or does not, structure American politics. He makes numerous references throughout his discussion to foreign threats. Yet what is perhaps most arresting in his discussion is how little attention he pays to a legalistic argument over war powers, prerogative powers, the few court cases that could be cited, or general theories of government. His attention is directed almost entirely toward the politics of presidential leadership that he found so evident in the early New Deal. They afforded Herring a series of practical maxims and principles derived from observation more than theoretical or legal reasoning.

With the danger of war imminent, "presidents cannot afford the luxury of fighting with Congress" as Wilson did at the end of his second term in the fight over the Treaty of Versailles.[57] Even if the president were successful, it would be a Pyrrhic victory at best. Absent consensus, leadership is not merely difficult but nearly impossible. "The effectiveness of a presidential appeal against the protest of Congress would depend upon the response of the nation."[58] It would be a theoretically easy task to redesign American government along parliamentary lines in order to concentrate executive power, but if such a concentration served merely to overwhelm legitimate opposition, it is not clear that such a concentration would serve the ultimate purposes of either the president or the common good, even in wartime. In a practical sense the problem of presidential leadership arrives at something of a stalemate just as it arrives at its most crucial test.

It is futile to argue that the Senate should be deprived of its treaty-ratifying power, and by way of extension, its war powers. The problem is not that of eliminating legislative influence in these matters, "but rather of gaining Congressional understanding and support in the whole sphere of foreign relations." Here Woodrow Wilson serves mainly as a bad example. "It is not enough to have a good policy: equally necessary is Congressional support. President Wilson's behavior in 1918 is the spectacular example of what not to do."[59] The liberal-progressive tradition of policy government had too often assumed that it was sufficient merely to present good ideas and then have them enforced and administered by experts in executive branch agencies. It assumed a degree of policy rationality and coherence that was driven more by economic than political calculation. Again, the exercise of war powers by the president requires that the political calculations of consensus building be increased and not diminished. "Without the votes presidential leadership is feckless."[60]

The system has its weaknesses, but the weaknesses sometimes mask certain inherent strengths: "To stand generally accountable for the whole, even though he lacks control over all the parts, a presidential commander in chief is elected for a four year term. Though battles may be lost, no provision is made for a better tactician until the sands of time have run their allotted course.... In halcyon times a discredited occupant of the White House is an inconvenience; in times of emergency such institutionalized futility may become tragic."[61] What saves the American system is, paradoxically, the elusive nature of accountability—a point that seemed to be a fatal weakness to the Wilsonian mind. Since responsibility is difficult to pinpoint, it is relatively easy for the president to shift the blame to someone else, which FDR did frequently whenever he seemed to be in trouble, and there never seems to be a lack of administration officials willing to fall on their swords to protect the president. But above all, perhaps, the system allows for the time necessary for a consensus war policy to emerge.

The ease with which presidents can shift the blame for their own failures onto someone else appears on the surface to be craven, but it has its uses. The English prime minister is so sensitive to public opinion that the work of a single day may cause his overthrow. On the face of it, executive power in Great Britain during the first year of World War II, first under the leadership of Neville Chamberlain and then Winston Churchill, was perhaps less stable than wartime leadership under Roosevelt. "The results of the British Conservative Party in encouraging German rearmament because of fear of Communism are now apparent. Parliamentary government does not provide a place in policy formation for all the parties of interest."[62] Roosevelt had to try to bribe, cajole, and twist an often reluctant Congress to follow his lead, and he was certainly was devious in his tactics, though not in his ultimate aims. This caused later critics of Roosevelt as a war leader to accuse him of engaging in a "backdoor to war," but Herring's analysis suggests a far different and more benign interpretation.[63] While Herring does not specifically address this later criticism, his analysis points to an institutional explanation. The nature of executive leadership in the American system will be different from the nature of executive leadership in a parliamentary system. In the American system, "[t]he president would cease to be effective if he had to bear this burden alone."[64] While Wilson and the progressive science of modern democracy preferred a parliamentary system for channeling executive leadership, Herring, after weighing the pros and cons, came down on the side of the American system. But it is difficult to find any normative reasons for his defense of democracy: His defense is essentially that "it works."

Presidential Leadership from the Founding to the Modern Presidency

Herring's defense of presidential leadership in the American system appears at first glance to be well within the tradition of Hamilton and "energy" as the engine of American government. But while he agreed with Hamilton that energy in the executive was consistent with popular government, he did so for very different reasons. He appears to have thought of his work as occupying a kind of halfway house between the abstract political science of both the founders and the liberal-progressive tradition of Woodrow Wilson. What links remain between his slender volume and *The Federalist* is that both are built on a broad and deep appreciation of the frailties and occasional nobility of the human character and how they play out in government. Madison remarked, accurately, "But what is government itself, but the greatest of all reflections on human nature?" (Fed. 51) In Herring's formulation of democratic consensus, he wrote, "If our democracy fails to meet the demands of the hour, the fault will not lie with the system but with ourselves. In the ultimate reckoning the governance of a free people is an affair not of forms but of men."[65] While it was clear to Herring that the form of government affected how leadership was exercised, it was equally clear that it was the leader who made the office: In this it was a decidedly un-Wilsonian understanding of political reform and much more akin to why the founders thought of George

Washington as the indispensable man—perhaps the only president who was considered a statesman before his death. Form was not, for either the Progressives or Herring, linked to the purpose of government. Herring shared with liberal-progressive scholarship a rejection of the founders' science of politics: What he did not share was its arguments in favor of a parliamentary system. But, by the time of the New Deal, it might be said that he differed from Wilson more in means than ends.

If there is a weakness in Herring's discussion of presidential leadership it may be rooted in the very qualities that give it strength: his insightful mastery of legislative politics and the personalities behind them. His focus on political behavior led him to depreciate the more philosophical defenses of republican government in the founders' political science. This helped fuel a critique of behavioralism by the new political science movement of the 1960s that it was merely a disguised defense of the status quo masquerading as objective analysis. What Herring's analysis of presidential leadership signaled to political scientists was the notion that presidential leadership could be studied independently of any significant constitutional structure. It was a deconstitutionalized study of American democracy.[66] The focus on "process" as opposed to symbolic substance gave weight to this charge.[67] In a sense the critics were right—it was more or less a defense of the existing political institutions of American government. But that did not make it "reactionary" with all of the pejorative connotations that term came to embody at a later date. In Herring's case, at least, it is more properly a mature defense of the American system as decidedly superior to anything to be found in the abstract thought of intellectuals. "The concept of 'experts' and that of 'people' are altogether too simple to prove useful for purposes of analysis," he wrote.[68] Again, he has a point. Herring broke with the Progressives on the notion that the form of government was a significant element in a science of politics, but he certainly agreed that government could be studied without reference to the natural rights arguments of the founding. Indeed, the very nature of his methodology changed the academic analysis of the separation of powers from a defense of political freedom to a more mundane issue of "guerrilla warfare" between two institutions of government, each motivated by what are essentially Machiavellian calculations. The moral calculus of leadership was not part of Herring's framework.

It is the absence of an explicit moral calculus in *Presidential Leadership* that is perhaps the most glaring omission of Herring's discussion of presidential leadership. He refuses to defend the constitutional system in the founders' language—the language of natural rights—for example. Natural rights have no place in Herring's political science lexicon and its absence affected his perception of presidential leadership. The purpose of his work was to create a science of politics that would be able to penetrate to the heart of American politics independent of the founders' political science. He accepted facts as they were revealed by research and assumed that such facts would somehow produce a theory of democracy more substantial than that of the founders.[69] The irony of his approach can be found in the inability of political science so narrowly defined to actually reach the heart of politics in terms either the founders or Progressives would understand. What, after all, is the purpose of presidential leadership if not to defend the polity as defined in the founding documents? The founders cast their arguments in terms of aims and purpose: Behavioralism studied process. Purpose tended, in this analytic context, to be tied to the personal qualities of whoever assumed a leadership position. The behavioral approach tended to study aspects of process that could be quantified and that meant, in turn, the study of numbers of various sorts. It is as if Herring's discovery of behavioral methodology somehow entailed the loss the founders' natural rights political science. In Herring's account, the Constitution and the philosophical arguments behind it were little more than the wallpaper of American politics: a background to the activity in the room that is the real object of political science. It is true that in any form of democracy it is important to know the numbers of people associated with opinions about things: Numbers often affect the process of government, especially a government founded on popular principles. But it is also important to know something about the motivations, principles, and political purposes those people behind the numbers hope to achieve. In the American regime, these questions are invariably tied to the founding principles.

Purpose does not disappear simply because there is a reluctance to talk about it: It merely goes underground, and when it resurfaces, as it eventually will, it may come as a surprise to a science of politics unable to analyze it. The absence of purpose makes politics appear small and an affair of tremendous trifles. Such, at any rate, was not the founders' view of politics, and, ultimately, it was not Herring's either, although he found it difficult to express himself in the natural rights language of the Declaration of Independence. And as with any faculty that is not exercised, inactivity tends to produce atrophy. In this case, what is atrophied is thinking about the purpose of politics. Even if the founders are mistaken about the purpose of politics, they remain the standard against which the American regime is typically measured. Roosevelt, correctly or not, cast his New Deal as the progressive fulfillment of the "American dream," by which he meant to link the New Deal with the founding principles of the regime. Had he failed to do so, it is doubtful either his policies or his presidency would be remembered as they are.

Curiously for a work on presidential leadership, especially one that is written in the context of the presidency of Franklin Roosevelt, there is no extended discussion, or even a mention, of any charismatic qualities that might be important to a calculus of how presidents lead. Herring's analysis remains perhaps the best analytic discussion of institutional politics during the New Deal. And it is written with a literary flair that no doubt reflects his undergraduate degree in literature from Johns Hopkins. He closed his Foreword to *The Politics of Democracy* with a pithy quote from Chaucer and spiced each chapter heading in his *Public Administration and the Public Interest* with quotes from *Alice in Wonderland,* none of which was filched from Bartlett's *Familiar Quotations.* But energy in the office of president as Herring described it was not, as it was for Hamilton, or even Madison and Jefferson, something tied to constitutional inter- pretation. It was closer to the political science of the Progressives in the sense that it regarded the founding arguments as anti- quated. In that sense it might be understood as a logical out- growth of the political science of the Progressive Era even if it departed from it in some significant ways. It departed from the Progressives in the sense that it regarded all arguments over constitutional form to be essentially meaningless. Political be- havior was certainly affected by institutions, but not as much as it was affected by the personalities of the politicians themselves.

But neither the founding arguments over presidential power nor the liberal-progressive challenge expressed by Woodrow Wilson can or should be dismissed too lightly. For better or worse, they each embodied a principle of how a popular form of government *ought* to operate. Each understood process but also understood purpose as well. The founders and the Progressives had each sought to ground presidential leadership in the moral authority of the president. A full understanding of the quarrel between the Progressives and the founders would require a separate analysis of how they understood moral authority in government and cannot be discussed here. The problem with Herring's behavioralism was not that it was lacking in genuine insights on how presidential leadership operates in the American system, but that it presented a much too tepid defense of popular government in crisis times. In crisis times it may not be enough merely to ward off an evil: What is also required is to actively defend the good that is in the regime, if such there is. Leadership in crisis times requires appeals to "our better angels" and not merely to our worst fears. In turn, this means a rediscovery of such terms as "prudence," "judgment," "right" and "wrong," and, when appropriate, "good" and "evil." In the American scheme of politics, such appeals will invariably be tied to the natural rights origins of the regime or they are likely to fall on barren soil. Herring appreciates prudential knowledge in politicians, but he never links prudence to purpose beyond the most immediate calculations. It is surely one of the essential elements in presidential leadership that we recognize the moral authority in both the office and the individual who happens to occupy it at any particular point in time.[70]

The behavioral approach to politics that Herring helped to pioneer explicitly focused on the practical side of politics. In a sense, there is nothing wrong with this. As Aristotle pointed out, politics is particularly the realm of practical knowledge as opposed to theoretical knowledge. And statesmanship requires a prudential judgment about practical matters that theoretical reasoning does not. But prudential judgment is judgment about means and ends, and presidents in particular, if they are ever to be judged as statesmen, need to understand both. The analysis of process is, by its very nature, an analysis of means. And an analysis of means without an appreciation of ends is unlikely to yield a very satisfactory understanding even of means: It will be an incomplete science of politics precisely for that reason. The practical reasoning of politics invariably involves at least implicit knowledge of ends. Practical reasoning can only be interpreted and evaluated in terms of the ends pursued. The institutional analysis so well represented by Herring's work lacks any reference to the ends of government. The students of American politics who have routinely rated Franklin Roosevelt as one of America's "great" presidents have typically based their judgment on the ends of the New Deal as the creation of the modern welfare state very much along the lines begun by the Progressives. Herring did not disagree with that perspective, but neither did he elaborate upon it.

The founders cast their arguments for republican government in the language of what they called a "new science of politics" because they were confident in the moral purpose that lay behind their claims. They were claims based on a political reasoning associated with natural rights. Behavioralism, on the other hand, is a political science of process: of means rather than ends. The absence of an explicit defense of purpose in government is most likely to mean that process is viewed as an empty vessel into which any particular liquid may be poured without destroying its essential function. Herring was very much aware that there was more to politics than process. But his analysis was tethered to a methodology that had no room for moral purpose. This is not the place to retrace the steps of Leo Strauss in deploring the disappearance of the natural rights tradition of the Declaration of Independence in American political science.[71] It is sufficient to point out that the contemporary inability to explore any moral purpose in contemporary politics has left it open to various critiques of the founders that would, if carried out, probably destroy regime principles. Even the most prudential presidential leadership under these circumstances is open to challenge because there is no idea of what proper presidential leadership ought to be. The artificial distinction between facts and values then becomes an impediment to a complete regime analysis, much less to its defense. Before we can know with any certainty whether or not any particular institution is functioning properly, we first need to know what it is supposed to do. This is why facts and values are inseparable both in theory and practice.

It is doubtful if anyone has more systematically explored the politics of Roosevelt's New Deal than Pendleton Herring. What makes his work even more remarkable is that the passage of time has not dramatically increased our knowledge of the process more than the account Herring has bequeathed to us. As a case study of presidential leadership in crisis times, Herring's work is a masterpiece of its kind. But his methodology was so tied to time, place, and circumstance that we are left to wonder about the lessons of history. Herring seems to be conflicted on this score himself. The irony of his analysis of presidential leadership is that at the end of his account we may not know much more about that elusive quality than we did at the outset. Leadership depends on personality, political skill, time, place, and circumstance. We at least think we know that the constitutional ordering of institutions does not prevent presidential leadership, as Wilson thought, and we may realize that the founders' system has some advantages over a parliamentary system. We can describe presidential leadership in action, but we cannot really be certain if it is leadership or merely cynical maneuvering for personal advantage. We are left to wonder whether presidential leadership can be compartmentalized this easily, between practical skills on the one hand and moral virtues on the other: whether a satisfactory science of politics without reference to ends is even possible. None of this should detract from the study of political process, especially in crisis times as Herring did it. Such studies serve as guideposts that mark how the American regime has developed and how it has changed at critical junctures. Marking these developments is, at any rate, a good day's work for any political scientist.

SIDNEY A. PEARSON, JR.
Radford University, Virginia

Notes

[1] Hamilton's contribution on this point is not diminished even though, as Charles Thach pointed out, "the executive of the Constitution is not traceable to Hamilton's contributions." See Charles C. Thach, Jr., *The Creation of the Presidency 1775-1789: A Study in Constitutional History* (Baltimore: The Johns Hopkins Press, 1923), p. 94.

[2] Adrienne Koch (Ed.), *Notes of Debates in the Federal Convention of 1787 Reported by James Madison* (Athens, Ohio: Ohio University Press, 1966), esp. pp. 135-136.

[3] See the fine discussion of the place of behavioralism in the development of modern American political science in David M. Ricci, *The Tragedy of Political Science: Politics, Scholarship, and Democracy* (New Haven: Yale University Press, 1984).

[4] Raymond Tatalovich and Thomas S. Engeman, *The Presidency and Political Science: Two Hundred Years of Constitutional Debate* (Baltimore, Maryland: The Johns Hopkins University Press, 2003). Tatalovich and Engeman have traced in fine detail, through an impressive selection of significant works on the presidency, responses to Hamilton's sketch of executive power in *The Federalist*.

[5] Perhaps the best example of this is James MacGregor Burns, *Roosevelt: The Lion and the Fox* (New York: Harcourt, Brace, and Company, 1956). Burns openly embraced the famous Machiavellian metaphor in his study of Roosevelt and incorporated it into the title of the first volume of his work. All of the founders, it seems safe to say, would have found such an open association a horror, even as it would have no doubt confirmed the worst fears of the Anti-Federalists.

[6] See Woodrow Wilson's review of James Bryce, *The American Commonwealth* (1888), in Ray Stannard Baker and William E. Dodd (Eds.), *College and State: Educational, Literary, and Political Papers (1875-1913)*, Vol. 1 (New York: Harper & Brothers, 1925), pp. 159-178.

[7] This is the theme of Harvey C. Mansfield, Jr., *Taming the Prince: The Ambivalence of Modern Executive Power* (New York: The Free Press, 1989).

[8] See my "Reinterpreting the Constitution for a New Era: Woodrow Wilson and the Liberal-Progressive Science of Politics," in Woodrow Wilson, *Constitutional Government in the United States* (New Brunswick, New Jersey: Transaction Publishers, 2002). Hereafter cited as *CG*.

[9] The Progressive reaction to Hamilton was ambiguous, prompted in large part by their general critique of the founders as a whole. See Stephen F. Knott, *Alexander Hamilton and the Persistence of Myth* (Lawrence, Kansas: The University Press of Kansas, 2002), esp. ch. 5.

[10] John A. Rohr, *To Run a Constitution: The Legitimacy of the Administrative State* (Lawrence, Kansas: University Press of Kansas, 1986).

[11] See for example, Frank J. Goodnow, *Politics and Administration: A Study in Government* (New York: The Macmillan Company, 1900).

[12] The best single treatment of political science in the Progressive Era is Dennis J. Mahoney, *Politics and Progress: The Emergence of American Political Science* (Lanham, Maryland: Rowman & Littlefield, 2004).

[13] Herbert Croly, *The Promise of American Life*. Edited by Arthur M. Schlesinger, Jr. (Cambridge, Massachusetts: The Belknap Press, 1965), p. 214.

[14] William Howard Taft, *Our Chief Magistrate and His Powers*. With a Foreword and Introductory Notes by H. Jefferson Powell (Durham, North Carolina: Carolina Academic Press, 2002). Powell's very fine introduction is especially helpful in getting straight what Taft did and did not advocate in his exchange with Roosevelt.

[15] E. Pendleton Herring, *Public Administration and the Public Interest* (New York: McGraw-Hill Book Company, Inc., 1936).

[16] The best account of this movement is Theodore Rosenof, *Realignment: The Theory That Changed the Way We Think About American Politics* (Lanham, Maryland: Rowman & Littlefield, 2003).

[17] See the interview of Pendleton Herring by Fred Greenstein in Michael A. Baer, Malcolm E. Jewell, and Lee Siegelman (Eds.), *Political Science in America: Oral Histories of a Discipline* (Lexington, Kentucky: The University Press of Kentucky, 1991), pp. 22-39.

[18] See my "Public Opinion and *The Pulse of Democracy*," *Society*, November-December 2004, pp. 56-70.

[19] Pendleton Herring, "On the Study of Government," *American Political Science Review*, Vol. XLVI, December 1953, No. 4, p. 963.

[20] Pendleton Herring, *The Politics of Democracy: American Parties in Action* (New York: Rinehart & Company, Inc., 1940). His critique of Wilson and the disciplined view of parties are cogently argued in this work, pp. 100-116.

[21] See the insightful comments by Tatalovich and Engeman on the "heroic presidency" thesis in American political science, op. cit.

[22] Pendleton Herring, "American Government and Politics: Second Session of the Seventy-second Congress, December 5, 1932, to March 4, 1933," *American Political Science Review*, Vol. 27, No. 3 (June 1933), p. 415.

[23] Pendleton Herring, "American Government and Politics: First Session of the Seventy-third Congress, March 9, 1933, to June 16, 1933," *American Political Science Review*, Vol. 28, No. 1 (February 1934), p. 65.

[24] Pendleton Herring, "American Government and Politics: Second Session of the Seventy-third Congress, January 3, 1934, to June 18, 1934," *American Political Science Review*, Vol. 28, No. 5 (October 1934), p. 852.

[25] Ibid., p. 854.

[26] Ibid., p. 864.

[27] Ibid., p. 865.

[28] Pendleton Herring, "American Government and Politics: First Session of the Seventy-fourth Congress, January 3, 1935, to August 26, 1935," *American Political Science Review*, Vol. 29, No. 6 (December 1935), p. 1005.

[29] Pendleton Herring, *Presidential Leadership: The Political Relations of Congress and the Chief Executive* (New York: Reinhart & Company, 1940), p. ix. Hereafter cited as *PL*.

[30] Ibid., p. 52.

[31] Ibid., p. 1.

[32] Richard E. Neustadt, *Presidential Power: The Politics of Leadership* (New York: John Wiley & Sons, 1961). Neustadt briefly acknowledged Herring's contribution to his own thesis but, in my judgment, did not give sufficient credit to Herring. A wide-ranging discussion of Neustadt's thesis, along with its implications for the study of the presidency can be found in Robert Y. Shapiro, Martha Joynt Kumar, and Lawrence R. Jacobs (Eds.), *Presidential Power: Forging the Presidency for the Twenty-first Century* (New York: Columbia University Press, 2000). A recent challenge to Neustadt's thesis on its own terms is William G. Howell, *Power Without Persuasion: The Politics of Direct Presidential Action* (Princeton: Princeton University Press, 2003).

[33] *PL*, pp. 2-3.

[34] Ibid., p. 3. The best discussion of this point in the founders' system of presidential selection and its subsequent development is James W. Ceaser, *Presidential Selection: Theory and Development* (Princeton: Princeton University Press, 1979).

[35] Ibid., pp. 3-4. See Wilson, *CG*, pp. 54-81.

[36] This is perhaps most conspicuous in Robert Dahl in one of the earliest behavioral works that explored the founders' political science, *A Preface to Democratic Theory* (Chicago: The University of Chicago Press, 1956). A half century of scholarship and critique of his reading did not change Dahl's mind on the subject as is evidenced in his *How Democratic is the Constitution?* (New Haven: Yale University Press, 2001). The best specific critique of Dahl remains

M.J.C. Vile, *Constitutionalism and the Separation of Powers* (Clarendon Press; Oxford, 1967). See also Bradford P. Wilson and Peter W. Schramm (Eds.), *Separation of Powers and Good Government* (Lanham, Maryland: Rowman & Littlefield, 1994).

[37] *PL.*, p. 7.

[38] Ibid., p. 7.

[39] Ibid., p. 9.

[40] Ibid., p. 10.

[41] Ibid., p. 73.

[42] Ibid., p. 15.

[43] Ibid., p. 21.

[44] Ibid., p. 47.

[45] Ibid., p. 94.

[46] Ibid., 29.

[47] Ibid., p. 67-69.

[48] See my discussion of the "responsible party" school in American political thought in "E. E. Schattschneider and the Quarrel Over Parties in American Democracy," in E. E. Schattschneider, *Party Government: American Government in Action* (New Brunswick, New Jersey: Transaction Publishers, 2003), pp. ix-lviii.

[49] *PL.*, p. 53.

[50] Ibid., p. 37.

[51] Pendleton Herring, *The Politics of Democracy: American Parties in Action* (New York: W. W. Norton & Company, 1965), p. xi. The original edition of this work appeared in 1940.

[52] Ceaser, op. cit., esp. p. 22.

[53] *PL*, p. 45.

[54] The most formidable case for this thesis was advanced in 1966 by Aaron Wildavsky as "The Two Presidencies," in Aaron Wildavsky, *The Beleaguered Presidency* (New Brunswick, New Jersey: Transaction Publishers, 1991). A follow-up discussion of Wildavsky's thesis can be found in Steven A. Shull (Ed.), *The Two Presidencies: A Quarter Century Assessment* (Chicago: Nelson-Hall Publishers, 1991). Wildavsky also updated his original thesis with a few additional points in Richard Ellis and Aaron Wildavsky, *Dilemmas of Presidential Leadership: From Washington Through Lincoln* (New Brunswick, New Jersey: Transaction Publishers, 1989).

[55] *PL.*, p. 71.

[56] A full discussion of the founders' understanding of foreign affairs cannot and need not be discussed here. The best, and I think correct, constitutional perspective of the founders' in this context is H. Jefferson Powell, *The President's Authority Over Foreign Affairs: An Essay in Constitutional Interpretation* (Durham, North Carolina: Carolina Academic Press, 2002).

[57] Ibid., p. 51.

[58] Ibid., p. 75.

[59] Ibid., p. 87. See also Herring's pertinent comments on Wilson as a bad example of how to build an executive cabinet, p. 98.

[60] Ibid., p. 90.

[61] Ibid., p. 111-112.

[62] Ibid., pp. 128-129.

[63] The most powerful advocate of this thesis is Charles C. Tansil, *Back Door to War: The Roosevelt Foreign Policy, 1933-1941* (Chicago: University of Chicago Press, 1952). See also, Charles A. Beard, *President Roosevelt and the Coming of the War 1941: A Study in Realities and Appearances* (New Haven: Yale University Press, 1948).

[64] *PL.*, p. 115.

[65] Ibid., p. 146.

[66] The significance of a deconstitutionalized study of American democracy is nicely captured in Roger Barrus, John H. Eastby, Joseph H. Lane, Jr., David E. Marion, and James F. Pontuso, *The Deconstitutionalization of America: The Forgotten Frailties of Democratic Rule* (Lanham, Maryland: Lexington Books, 2004).

[67] Rosenof, op. cit.

[68] *PL.*, 116.

[69] Ricci, op. cit., pp. 110-111.

[70] On this point, see the stimulating series of essays in Moorhead Kennedy, R. Gordon Hoxie, and Brenda Repland (Eds.), *The Moral Authority of Government: Essays to Commemorate the Centennial of the National Institute of Social Sciences* (New Brunswick, New Jersey: Transaction Publishers, 2000).

[71] Leo Strauss, *Natural Right and History* (Chicago: The University of Chicago Press, 1953). See also Strauss' comments in Herbert J. Storing (Ed.), *Essays on the Scientific Study of Politics* (New York: Holt, Rinehart and Winston, Inc., 1962).

★ ★ ★ ★ ★ ★

Acknowledgments

THE AID of the Committee on Research in the Social Sciences at Harvard University is gratefully acknowledged.

For permission to use several passages from articles on Congress prepared on past occasions for the *American Political Science Review,* thanks are tendered to the editors of this journal.

The author is particularly grateful for the assistance received at various stages in the preparation of the manuscript from George Berquist, Harryette Cohn, and Roland Young. Louis Hartz was of great help in preparing data on the war powers of the president and in reading the manuscript. To the editor of this series, Professor Phillips Bradley, especial acknowledgment is due for criticism and suggestions. To the numerous officials who gave so generously of their time in discussing various problems raised in this book the reader as well as the author may feel a sense of indebtedness.

P. H.

Cambridge, Massachusetts
September, 1940

Preface

TODAY the federal government is called upon to act vigorously and quickly. We look to the president for leadership, yet we face new tasks with old political equipment.

One heritage of the past that today is central in any effort to adapt our governmental machinery to present problems is the idea of checks and balances and the separation of powers. These concepts are so deep that they are part of our folkways. The practical question is how to work through and around such assumptions, for this is no time to overhaul our political structure.

This book attempts to analyze the way in which our system works rather than to propound some substitute for it. The questions posed by the separation of powers are discussed only in so far as the president and the Congress are concerned. Many able writers have already dealt with the place of the courts and of judicial review. The relations between the president and Congress, especially their more purely political contacts in distinction to their legal powers, warrant examination, for here is the front line of attack upon those dangers which, if not satisfactorily dealt with, threaten our whole system of rule by law and government by discussion. The courts must do their part in defending judicial continuity and reconciling with precedent through the mysteries of jurisprudence the advances made in public policy. But the executive and legislative branches, impelled by the pressure of events, must venture forward into the unknown. Unless they succeed in their joint adventure, we may be overwhelmed by the weight of our own destiny.

Sometimes it seems a wonder that the machine creaks along at all. In looking at the operation of Congress and the executive we may see with Ezekiel,

> De little wheel run by faith,
> And de big wheel run by de grace ob God,
> 'Tis a wheel in a wheel,
> Way in de middle ob de air.

Yet, if our tasks are to be done, the two wheels of government must be geared together, put in rapid motion, and given firm direction by free men. This is no simple accomplishment, but a critical analysis of recent experience points clearly to the fundamental soundness of our system of government for meeting the future. Since this success depends upon the way in which the governmental machine is handled, an explanation of the methods and conditions of presidential leadership is pertinent. We face a world where discipline, organization, and the concentration of authority are placed before freedom for the individual and restraints on government. Internal economic problems likewise call for a greater degree of continuity and consistency in public policy. Yet our government was originally designed for no such complex necessities.

What can we do with what we have? Can our government meet the challenge of totalitarianism and remain democratic?

Is the separation of powers between the legislative and executive branches compatible with the need for authority? In seeking firm leadership do we open ourselves to the danger of dictatorship? These pressing questions of the hour warrant a fresh examination of the relations between the president and Congress.

Presidential Leadership

Chapter I

The Political Basis of Presidential Power

THE president is a figure symbolic of national purpose: he is also a human being. The kind of man he shows himself to be is intimately related to the power and meaning he gives his office. Hence there are few common characteristics of all presidents. Perhaps the chief constant is that the president must prove successful as a politician before he can attain this highest elective office. Whether he proves to be a statesman depends more upon the historians than upon the voters. The people elect the president, but they are not organized to support him in office: it is to Congress that he must constantly turn for the fulfillment of his objectives.

To talk of the president as the "people's choice" is to use extremely loose language. Viewed in terms of what actually takes place at elections, the "people's choice" is usually the man who succeeds in winning through a sectional alliance barely enough votes to gain the presidency. Once ensconced, he is fortified by the symbols and associations of his high office and at least during the first few years of his term is regarded as the tribune of the people. Actually he is the product of a combination of political circumstances. He is selected in the first instance by the union of legerdemain and popular enthusiasm which is practiced in our national party conventions. Moreover, there is no guarantee that the political coalition which made his election possible will hold together long enough to carry through to consummation any program that may have been projected. The choice of a responsible chief executive by the general electoral process is the unique feature of our governmental system. The candidate appeals to the voters at large for his election, yet once in office he is dependent upon Congress for the realization of his program.

Congress is a heterogeneous group of individuals responsible to local machines and special interests; the president represents an over-all constituency whose mass verdicts often differ from the dictates of pure localism. To reconcile these two political patterns the president needs some means for controlling local party organizations. If a direct line can be established between the national headquarters of the party and the local political workers who do the daily work of politics, the president's chances of getting dependable support in Congress are greatly increased. Unless the president can offer substantial help in fighting local political battles, he cannot demand support from the congressmen from these localities. Since politicians must please the dominant elements in their districts, the chief executive must become a factor in local politics. He may accomplish this in part by the general prestige he enjoys; this is, however, a transitory influence and not likely to maintain the loyalty of the machines throughout his term. The president can often enhance his local strength through the use of patronage, but support won in this way is no more enduring than human gratitude nor is it stronger than the expectation of further favors.

We have created a position of great power but have made

the full realization of that power dependent upon influence rather than legal authority. Hence if our president is to be effective, he must be a politician as well as a statesman. He must consider the political expedience of contemplated actions as well as their consistency with his concept of the public interest.

The element of contingency in our system is inherent in the uncertainty of party programs and party discipline. We are apparently willing to give popular support to a president while at the same time rejecting some of his most cherished measures. The president is titular head of the nation, chief legislator, and chief representative, as well as chief executive; we do not necessarily support him in all roles at the same time.

As the original conception of the presidency was reflected in the electoral college, the man elected to the office was to be above party conflict. He would possibly in most cases be selected by the legislative body itself, and the existence of this process would mean a direct connection between him and the power electing him and enacting his program.

It does not necessarily follow, however, that the Founding Fathers were bent upon creating an ineffective executive. The deadlocks between Congress and the executive have been most serious when these two branches of government have been identified with different political parties. Thus while under some circumstances the political party serves to link the different branches of government, it may also be instrumental in creating an impasse. The party system results in both agreement and disagreement.

The Founding Fathers were not inviting constant stale-

mate when they subscribed to the Whig principle of checks
and balances. They did not, of course, anticipate that the
executive would be chosen by millions of voters or even by
the small percentage of persons possessing the franchise at
the time. The provisions which they wrote, while they are
anachronisms today, were nonetheless based upon a realistic
conception. The Revolution did not bring a widening of
the franchise: the conduct of the government remained in
the hands of the gentry. This ruling class possessed the confidence of the people and the participation of a broader
electorate only came slowly through the years. Under the
Constitution a class of men with common interests and a
common desire to maintain a central government found that
they could co-operate effectively.

In theory the president was to be selected from among the
class of wise and responsible men carrying the burden of
public affairs. Although the weaknesses of the scheme became only too quickly apparent, the plan itself must not be
dismissed as fantastic. It provided for an executive whose
authority was to rest upon the confidence and support of
that group which was most concerned with the conduct of
government. The president's power would thus have a definite basis—nonpartisan, but nonetheless politically significant.

Stable executive authority under any system requires a
substantial base. Kings have founded their authority upon
a loyal army, a faithful nobility, or a bureaucracy. Under a
parliamentary system the authority of the ministry is based
upon a party majority. Under our system the Constitution
provided that the choice of the president would devolve
upon the House of Representatives if the electors should
fail to agree. The president chosen in this event would have
as his basis of influence the factions dominating Congress,

and the source of his political power would be comparable to that of a prime minister even though his tenure was for a fixed term. The contingency which was not anticipated was the popular nomination and election of the chief executive, and the full political consequences of this development did not become apparent for several decades. Because of "presidential succession" and nomination by a Congressional caucus, the chief executive maintained a close relation with Congress. To the extent that he was the choice of the politicians controlling that body he could rely upon Congressional support after the election. And even when it became clear that the voters would not tolerate a chief executive who was merely the choice of the legislature, parties were not welcomed as devices for developing a working relationship between the two branches of government.

A fear of party government persisted for decades into the nineteenth century. Suspicion of a strong, independent executive was only one reason for the common view of the presidency. The framers of the Constitution were certainly not desirous of establishing a separation of powers as great as that which developed under a bipartisan system, but the broadening of the franchise introduced forces with which they had not reckoned. Much to the discomfiture of some good citizens the presidency became a prize fought for by rival political factions. Since this was regarded as a consequence of permitting the election of an executive by a general ticket, it was considered better to eliminate such contests than to encourage thereby the development of party government.[1]

Presidential government has, of course, developed too far for such protests to be pertinent, yet the system of a popu-

[1]Speeches in North Carolina Constitutional Convention of 1835, quoted in George D. Luetscher, *Early Political Machinery*, Philadelphia, 1903, pp. 113-14.

larly elected presidency failed to provide stable support for executive leadership. This was most marked in the relations between the president and Congress, since the extent of the executive's power was entrusted to the fortuitous circumstances determining the composition of the legislature.

The original constitutional provisions were contravened, but no efforts were made to adjust formally the relation of the two branches. Members of Congress were precluded by the Constitution from participating simultaneously in administrative duties, and the president lacked a dependable and legally constituted basis of political support. The Founding Fathers knew what kind of chief executive they wanted, and they made provisions for realizing their ideal. The president was to act as a moderator between the two houses of Congress; he was to stand above all factional differences; he was to arbitrate between men of conflicting views. Washington endeavored to fulfill this conception of the chief magistrate's function, and only in the light of bitter experience was this ideal modified. In the political theories of John Adams: "The emphasis is constantly placed upon the executive magistrate being the third power needed for the balance between the two assemblies, with function as mediator, arbitrator, arbiter, umpire, to mediate, intervene, interpose, and decide between the senate and the people, between the nobles and the commons, between the aristocracy and the democracy, between the rich and the poor, between the few and the many, in the two chambers, and between two parties, as we shall later see,—impartial, made so because his interest, for ultimate self-preservation, is to side with the weaker of the other two, whichever it may be at the time being."[2]

[2]Correa Moylan Walsh, *The Political Science of John Adams.* (New York: G. P. Putnam's Sons, 1915) 78–79.

Beginning with Jefferson and developing with Jackson, the general conception of the presidential office changed greatly.

Writers began to think of the chief executive less as a magistrate and more as a champion of the people. It was argued that presidential leadership is opposed by business interests: "The Tribune of the People stands guard against plutocracy." This is an oversimplification. There is a great temptation to seek a formula that will explain in some over-all fashion the periodic shifts from Congressional to presidential leadership and back again. To indulge in such ratiocination is to disregard the nature of the materials with which we are dealing. To attempt to isolate any one factor as responsible for executive leadership, or to picture Congressional dominance as persistently the effect produced by a given causation, is to impose an *a priori* frame of reference.

Observation discloses a succession of Congressional sessions and chief executives different in personal characteristics and in surrounding circumstances. The equipoise noted in any moment of time is the instant product of the interaction of the variable characteristics of the forces in conflict. With more or less plausibility, an observer may insist that in his judgment a particular outcome was due to an ascertainable set of causes. But to go further and argue that Congressional-executive relations are governed by certain specific forces is to substitute argumentation for observation. The uniformity of behavior that is clear is sufficient in itself. We see that political power shifts from the executive to the legislative branch and back again. Our system thus provides alternative institutional outlets, thereby facilitating the expression of changes in the political pattern of social forces in the country.

The doctrine of the separation of powers thus finds a realistic justification, not in a distinction of function between legislative and executive branches, but rather in providing that one branch will be open for contesting the control that has been previously established in the other branch. The Whig concept of a separation of power would lead to stalemate; this has sometimes happened. Politics is too dynamic for this sort of outcome to be maintained or endured. Fortunately, the institutions created under this Whig theory have in practice meant not a balance but an alternation of power. Under a parliamentary form of government the "loyal opposition" has stood ready to take office whenever the ministry in power lost the confidence of the representative assembly. Our federal system with fixed and staggered election periods and with an independent executive calls for different methods. Instead of a contest between two disciplined national parties we have in this country a battle between the localism and special interests represented in Congressional blocs and the broader interests of the community sporadically expressed by those presidents standing forth from time to time as "tribunes of the people." In this sense we can point to the centripetal forces converging in the chief executive and the centrifugal influences found in Congress. Positive presidential policy in time accumulates grievances and irritations; these find an outlet through Congressional criticism and ultimately counterweight executive power. Blocs become more insistent and intransigent in their opposition to the administration program. A president is usually discredited in Congress before he leaves office. Time and again a negative president follows a dynamic one. But negativity cannot be long endured, and the discontented seek a standard bearer once again.

Our system is able to reckon with this change of mode, this realignment of interests. We cannot predict content or timing, but the fact of periodicity is undeniable. If the relations between the president and Congress were not suited to this alternation, some other appropriate institutional device would have to be contrived.

Leadership in the making of public policy is fixed neither in the president nor in Congress. At some times the legislative branch of the government assumes major responsibility for charting the public course: at others the chief executive dominates the process. Through the radio and the press the president may seek to maintain his national constituency; but in the actual exercise of his power he must seek the day-to-day assent of the particularism of political forces represented in Congress and in local machines. The president is commonly thought of as representing the general welfare; Congress is the tool of "special interests." In fact presidential policy, however "pure" in motivation, must mean the promotion of certain interests at the expense of others. A recent example will illustrate the point. President Roosevelt's support of the St. Lawrence waterway meant that one part of the country would be benefited and other parts placed at a competitive disadvantage. The strong influence of sectionalism is clearly seen if the vote on the measure is considered. Strong opposition came from all states of the Atlantic seaboard region. The bill was ardently sponsored by the president, but party loyalty had little to do with the outcome (Dem. 31 yea, 22 nay; Rep. 14 yea, 20 nay; F.-L. 1 yea). In a special message to the Senate on January 10, 1934, the president said: "Broad national reasons lead me, without hesitation, to advocate the treaty. There are two main considerations —navigation and power."

Where the interests of their state were not affected, Democratic senators followed the president. For instance, the South Central states were generally favorable, but Long and Overton of Louisiana put New Orleans shipping first and opposed the bill. Of the ten senators from Ohio, Illinois, Michigan, Wisconsin, and Indiana, five were Republicans and five Democrats. Eight of the ten supported the president's bill, but the two Democratic senators from Illinois had local considerations of their own. The Senate vote of 46 to 42 failed to reach the two-thirds required for ratification.

What interests find it easiest to work through the Senate; which prefer to work through the House; which turn to the presidency? The president may serve as a leader-symbol to some people; to others he is simply one way to get things done.

The conflict between Congress and the president has often become accentuated and confused by the rather consistent interventionist policy advocated by the executive branch and the strong isolationist sentiment voiced by certain members of Congress. For example, a vigorous foreign policy is facilitated by allowing the president a free hand. Today we see the groups who bitterly fought the dictatorial methods of New Deal internal policy rallying in support of presidential initiative in foreign affairs.

In discussing the presidency the intensely personal nature of the office must never be overlooked. To treat the powers of the chief executive without reference to the individual incumbent is to ignore the chief determining factor. Woodrow Wilson pointed out that the office of president "has been one thing at one time, another at another."[3] Our Presidents can make much or little of their office.

An outline of the president's formal powers relating to Congress emphasizes the fact that his powers in large measure are extraofficial, informal, and political. Under the Constitution he is empowered to call special sessions of Congress, report to it on the state of the nation, suggest legislation, veto legislation, and adjourn Congress when the two houses cannot agree on an adjournment day.

The Constitution provides for annual sessions of Congress, with the opening date set at January 3 by the Twentieth Amendment. And in times of emergency, or for the consideration of urgent legislation, the president may call either of the houses, or both of them, into special session.

The Constitution vested in the president a power which has assumed considerable political significance in providing that "he shall from time to time give to the Congress information of the state of the Union, and recommend to their consideration such measures as he shall judge necessary and expedient. . . ." Powerful presidents have been able to make of these messages virtual mandates for Congressional action: they are invariably sent at the opening of Congressional sessions. Beyond the annual formal message the president may send special communications to Congress on particular problems. Franklin D. Roosevelt, for example, has often used this method of exerting influence on Congress. What is more, messages are often used by the president to shape public

[3]Woodrow Wilson, *Constitutional Government in the United States.* (New York: Columbia University Press, 1917) 69.

opinion or provoke public discussion; they have great potential value as devices for leadership. The formal legal powers over Congress granted by the Constitution reside chiefly in the veto power.

With several minor exceptions, Congressional enactments must be signed by the president before they can become law; and his veto can be overridden only by a two-thirds vote in each house. The president's veto power does not extend to the matter of Congressional adjournment, to proposed constitutional amendments, or to concurrent resolutions, the latter actually subject to veto but by practice immune. If the president neither signs nor vetoes a bill within the ten-day limit established by the Constitution, it automatically becomes law. If the president receives a bill from Congress less than ten days before adjournment, he may veto the bill by not acting upon it, a method, often used, which is called the "pocket veto." As a political dodge rather than as a legal power the president's threat of a veto may be used effectively to influence Congress in writing a law.

The president is usually considered both chief administrator and chief legislator—the former by virtue of his constitutional position and governmental trends, and the latter by popular expectation and the absence of co-ordinated leadership in Congress. The public expects the president to lead Congress; Congress is unable to produce coherence of direction to rival his. Yet in both these very important roles the president is confronted by vexatious problems, for Congress possesses something of the dog-in-the-manger attitude, unable to fill the roles successfully itself and at the same time unwilling to place full confidence in the president.

Though the president is chief administrator, Congress often makes governmental agencies accountable to itself rather than to him. There is the whole difficult problem of the relations between the president and the so-called independent regulatory commissions. There is the practical difficulty involved in the surveillance of agencies too numerous for the capacity of any single mind. While the presidential office has developed wide powers over administration since the beginning of the century, it still is far from being solely responsible for all the acts of officialdom.

The uncertainty of responsibility is the point upon which the relations between executive and legislature are most often criticized. Most critically does this uncertainty manifest itself in connection with governmental appropriations: the president's budget recommendations may be disrupted by congressmen with interests no wider than their own constituencies.

Moreover, time and again our system has made possible rivalries between the president and Congress for public support. This duality cannot be conjured away by institutional changes that would establish presidential control over Congress: the causes lie too deep for superficial remedies.

Both the grandeur and the pettiness of our federal government lie in the fundamental fact that our political system embraces a continent—hence the checks and balances that were incorporated in the Constitution in order to win acceptance for this great charter of compromises; hence the presence of limitations in many other forms during our history.

When any one combination of political or economic forces becomes intrenched, the whole system is endangered. The domination of the cotton planters over the South led on to the Civil War; a Northern plutocracy afterwards threatened to disinherit segments of the South and West by its financial control of the resources of these regions. The concept of checks and balances can never lack meaning for government in a society of divergent interests. Nor will a unity of social aims result simply through legally granting priority to the policy of any single branch of the government or economic dominance to any single class to the exclusion of other interests.

We can symbolize our national unity in the presidency, our sectional interests in the Senate, and our localisms in the House. We can look to the courts for the preservation of a degree of continuity and consistency in the social changes authorized through legal channels. We can provide in some measure for the expertness and specialization of treatment required in diverse areas of social activity through an efficient administrative service. But the general welfare can be advanced only through the plurality of interests associated severally with these different functions of government.

As a matter of political expediency there can be no question that at times strong presidential leadership is necessary. Politicians and editorial writers seem justified in arguing that for tactical purposes during periods of crisis this is the device by which the public interest is best served. For political theorists to go further, however, and to state as an absolute canon of sound government the identity of national welfare and presidential responsibility is to substitute an idealistic desire for order and unity for a scientific acceptance of the inescapably relative nature of all institutions freely responsive to shifting human desires.

Granting that the chief executive is the most effective rallying point for leadership, he lacks a dependable national political organization to stabilize his influence. Governmental authority is distributed among the courts, administrative agencies, and the houses of Congress; social controls of an unofficial sort are widespread and diversified. Yet many insistent problems of national defense and economic welfare call for consistent and continuous treatment. It is easier to indicate this need than to discover or apply the remedy.

Men are ruled by habit and directed by self-interest. Human inertia is the strongest factor that government must surmount. Proper public policy may be clearly suggested by the course of events, but the actual line followed will be determined by the interaction between the new events and existent public attitudes. Thus in 1939–40 the cables from Europe convinced the State Department that war in Europe was inevitable and increased defense preparation essential. Our ultimate policy was the product of this conviction as modified and delayed by the opinions of isolationists, interventionists, pacifists, warriors, and the inert mass of people who had given no previous thought to the problem. The threat of a seemingly remote situation to individual self-interest had to be made clear.

Our political system places tremendous faith in the capacity of the American people at times of crisis to subordinate self-interest to the nation's welfare. The federal government, to be effective, must have this widespread affirmation of unity.

In a time of crisis our government has ample powers: all governments must, indeed, possess them, if they would survive. But, if emergency means an increase in executive powers, the return to normal conditions is vastly facilitated by a reassertion of Congressional independence. Concentration of power can most readily be placed in the chief executive. Party battles which replaced one powerful president with another drawn from the opposite party would avail little. Our separation of powers means that a real demobilization can readily take place after war is over. Hence so long as our structure of government is maintained we need have little fear of Fascism's growing out of increased executive power. On the contrary, Fascism is most likely to develop from factionalism, discord, and weak democratic leadership.

The powers of the chief executive are ample for war or the imminence of war. A systematic statement of the president's statutory war powers is offered in the appendix of this book. There is always the possibility that Congress may enact a general mobilization plan and thereby concentrate full powers in the executive for utilizing the entire resources of the nation in a war effort. As a broad answer to questions concerning the source of presidential power, Newton D. Baker's reply to a Congressional inquiry is in point. Said he: "Well, the place to look for it, sir, is first to read the description of the President of the United States, as Commander in Chief of the Army and Navy, and then in the decisions of the Supreme Court. There is no definition of it; there is no donation of it, but the Supreme Court has found it in abundance."[4]

Presidential powers in times of emergency really rest upon the imperative of events. Legal considerations have little meaning. One question that has been much debated in the past is how far Congress should go in formally abdicating its powers to the President in wartime.

James G. Randall, in his study of *Constitutional Problems under Lincoln,* notes that "most of Wilson's powers, in fact,

[4] B. M. Baruch, *Taking the Profits Out of War.* (Privately printed) 78.

were derived from Congressional authorization; while Lincoln's most conspicuous acts were without legislative authority."[5]

The American Legion has sponsored a universal draft and wartime price-fixing measure that would virtually center complete powers in the chief executive. The minority views of the Senate report state in part

Whether it will be a socialistic dictatorship set up under this bill, as is feared by the Chicago Tribune (which says that it opens the doors for the commissars), or whether it will be a Fascist, authoritarian, big-business-plus-Army-machine dictatorship, as the liberal and labor papers fear, no one can say now. It depends on whether we have a President who has socialistic leanings or a President who has ideas of treating the people tough in the interests of property.[6]

What kind of a man do we want in the White House? What personal leanings do we prefer? He may be pushed far in one direction or another by the pressure of events. His utter personal loyalty to democratic values would be our greatest safeguard. Lincoln was denounced as a dictator yet as Randall states: "no undue advantage was taken of the emergency to force arbitrary rule upon the country or to promote personal ends."[7] Political opposition continued; the voters were free to repudiate their president at the polls if they chose. His power remained contingent upon popular support. There is nothing "undemocratic" about such executive power. Fascism looms only when opposition is no longer admitted as legitimate.

[5] James G. Randall, *Constitutional Problems under Lincoln.* (New York: D. Appleton-Century Company, 1936) 524.

[6] Senate Report, No. 480 on S. 25, 75th Congress, 1st Session, p. 23.

[7] Randall, *op. cit.*, p. 521.

Preparation for defense requires planning and increased governmental control; war today means that the total economy is regulated and directed by the government. The presidential office is the keystone, but underneath there is no systematic organizational support through a disciplined national party. Congress cannot be coerced by the chief executive. Evidence on these points will be presented in later chapters. The supreme task of presidential leadership is to carry us along the road of planning and controls that must be traversed in a world of totalitarian economies while at the same time maintaining the democratic values for which all our sacrifice is made. This difficult task can only be accomplished through recognizing that a free people are capable of responding to their government's call. If our leaders resort to coercive legislation in all instances and rely upon official ukases for obtaining results, they may get action but they will at the same time lose the very values that they were supposed to safeguard. The strength of democratic leadership lies in the spontaneous loyalty of its followers. This is the strongest basis for presidential leadership.

Democracy can exist only in an atmosphere of tolerance; it can function only through widespread mutual confidence. A most dangerous charge to apply to one's opponent in a political campaign is the epithet "Fascist"! To read out the "loyal opposition" is to bring in a one-party system. It is the end of democratic government, whatever the partisan symbols or verbalisms may be. Democracy can mean government of the people, by the people, and for the people only in a symbolic sense. It is sheer poetry and to be treasured for that reason. But when democracy is analyzed, not in the language of its high prophets but in terms of its behavior, we observe that it is a system and an attitude of mind that tolerates many elites in many groups jostling and struggling. To the democrat, bureaucracy and plutocracy are equally distasteful. Yet hierarchy and centralization are inescapable components of our civilization. Freedom today may mean little more than an opportunity to choose our masters, but this is no small privilege. Thus diversity is as integral to democracy as totalitarianism is to dictatorship, but for this diversity to survive it must be capable of an implicit unity of response when antithetical systems threaten its very foundations. This view may seem to imply that our democratic assumptions are founded on a fatal paradox; by contrast, however, the assumptions of totalitarianism are so insecure that they must be constantly supported by terror and violence. Despite the theories of dictators, the fact of human diversity remains. This reality they dare not face. Their whole system is constructed on the premise that men blindly and unprotestingly follow *Der Fuehrer*. No alternative is admitted. Democratic governments are not driven to such mystical heights for loyalty or to the depths of terrorism for its enforcement. We depend on no fairy tales of a classless society, ruled only by good fairies in the name of the proletariat or of the state. Our forms of government are none too tidy, but neither is the pattern of our national life. Today there is plenty of evidence that we can recognize a democratically workable political order. Thus far few of us have reached for the Fasces wrapped in the slick cellophane of specious efficiency, but will we continue to hold to our political institutions, smooth from the familiar touch of long usage? Or will our penchant for mechanical gadgets carry over into politics? There are demagogues in this country who are shrewd political salesmen!

Presidential leadership is effective only in so far as the great majority of the voters freely give their support to the chief executive. The democratic heritage imposes this supreme gamble on the wisdom and good will of our fellow citizens: that our sense of national unity and common purpose will provide the basis for action in times of emergency.

In normal times bargaining is commonly characteristic of politics. At times of real crisis such bargains may be too dear. Then the conduct of public affairs must rise higher than a haggle. Our system is based on the not too exalted belief that in times of real emergency the individual will realize that his own self-interest is identical with the common welfare. Our democracy is not dependent for its continuance upon any greater idealism. As Ben Franklin put it: if we don't hang together we may hang separately. Presidential leadership can be effective only if we choose the former alternative. A dictator relies upon his secret police, his party, and his army; a prime minister is effective so long as he maintains the support of a majority of the representative assembly; our chief executive must hold the confidence of the nation.

Chapter II

Congressional Behavior

Oᴜʀ national legislative assembly is still a continental Congress. As the representative agency of a great continent it embraces a great variety of interests. If such a body is to function effectively, some degree of direction and control is essential. Our party system has not provided sufficient agreement on principles to dictate policy. Party discipline is limited—when it has been effective a strong president has directed Congressional leaders.

While the presidential office has provided the most effective focal point for national policy within our system, it would be a vast oversimplification to assume that by virtue of his *influence* the president also has *control* as well. Events, time and again, have given evidence of the extremely precarious hold that the president has over his following. Despite the growth in the power of the presidency and the advances for handling its duties that have been made, the chief executive's relations with Congress remain uncertain and sporadic.

Our legislative system tends to play into the hands of lobbyists. Professional manipulators can exploit the intricacy of the lawmaking process to forward their own ends. They can grasp every opportunity to befog public sentiment, isolate and bully members of Congress, and play off both sectional rivalries and jealousies between the two houses of Congress.

On the face of these facts the president is forced by the circumstances of his position to be as much of a manipulator as a leader. He must curb the more extreme demands of regional groups and classes. These elements appear in Congressional blocs backed by organized minorities concerned only with their immediate welfare. To evoke a unified conception of national interest from such warring forces would be difficult under any circumstances, and under our system proves at times well-nigh impossible.

In periods of peace we sacrifice to the expression of our conflicting desires the fruits that might come through planning and constructive policy. The price is heavy. Much economic well-being is thrown away through failure to set aside group interests in seeking a broader social good. Neither in the presidential office nor in the Congressional leaders does sufficient authority reside for imposing the discipline needed to offset the fear of sectional and group interests. The administration often does little more than keep order in the bread line that reaches into the Treasury.

All in all, Congressional behavior shows that "political pickings" may at times be reduced to bones of contention. Filibusters, deadlocked conference committees, party splits, non record votes, lobbyists—all contribute to the confusion of the lawmaking process. The pages of the *Congressional Record* which set out the details add poignancy to the motto, "In God We Trust"!

Despite federalism, bicameralism, factionalism, and the negative character of our political parties, the present governmental structure has been called upon to meet a national crisis. The president is expected to exercise responsible executive leadership. For sanction, he must rely in large measure upon the popular support engendered by the emergency. Yet even the pressure of a great crisis may not be sufficient to solidify the mosaic of our political diversity. Members of Congress in the past have not responded readily to party controls. Certainly the chairman of the party's national committee has not been able to coerce congressmen into following party plans. When attempted, such dictation has usually met with prompt protest. The party platform carries no weight that congressmen will accept. Congressman Luce has frankly written of the platform: "No thoughtful legislator feels himself bound by the make-weights thrown in to catch a few stray votes."[1]

Our party structure is not contrived to provide leadership in policy. Not only are the party organizations in the forty-eight states largely independent of each other, but, within states having the direct primary system, partisan control is also tenuous.

If a party is to be held responsible for the enactment of a legislative program, there must be a sufficient concentration of power in the party leaders to enable them to hold their following in line. One effective means is to permit party leaders to determine who should be nominated as representatives of the party. This is a key power sometimes disregarded in discussions of cabinet responsibility under parliamentary government. If we were ready to abolish direct primaries and grant to the national party organization the initial selection of Congressional candidates the disagreements between exe-

[1]Robert Luce, *Legislative Procedure*. (Boston: Houghton Mifflin Company, 1922) 504.

cutive and legislative branches would become insignificant and few. Our problems would be translated to a different area. Control of the national party machine would be the great prize. Another concomitant of strongly organized parties is a more definite partisan ideology. The pragmatic and often opportunistic attitudes habitually adopted by the major parties are congenial to their present loose-jointed structures.

Lacking the sanction of institutional controls or the stimulus of a party creed, we are thrown back upon the politics of persuasion and manipulation. Hence party control is principally used in heading off bloc demands. The formulation of a program has been left to the president and his informal advisers.

The intellectual leadership of the New Deal has not been in Congress. The politicians in the strategic posts won through long service in Congress were expected to follow the lead of idea men in the administrative branch. Party loyalty was supposed to hold congressmen in line behind a group of intellectuals who personally scorned the dictates of partisanship.

If resistance is encountered in maintaining procedural controls in Congress, vastly more difficulty is found in making party controls effective outside Congress. The so-called "purge" of 1938 demonstrated that the voters in the districts of the purgees were insistent on making their own choices at the voting booth. This is an obvious fact, but its implications go deep. One consequence is that the chief executive is denied the possibility of building up a unified party held together by common profession to a program or set of principles. The president's objectives are left without organizational support.

President Roosevelt and his New Deal advisers are clearly dissatisfied with this situation. In the elections of 1938 the president sought as members of Congress men who would support his measures; he also wanted as members of the Democratic party voters who believed in his brand of liberalism. He stubbornly persisted even in the face of self-predicted defeat. Thus, in August, 1938, he drew from a sealed envelope his own pre-election prophecy that Olin D. Johnston, whom he had opposed, would be elected governor of South Carolina. Not only in this state, but in Maryland and Idaho, presidential interference played into the hands of anti-Roosevelt candidates. The battle cannot be explained, however, in terms of opposing schools of thought. Machine rivalries and undercover manipulation contributed to the results. Moreover, in several instances, notably in Kentucky, the support of W.P.A. workers strengthened the New Deal. In consequence the Hatch Act was passed partly as a means of counteracting the national support of federal job holders. Another act in the drama was played at the Chicago Convention in July, 1940, when the New Dealers overrode the conservative faction of the Democratic party. Here was a notable step in the president's effort to obtain a national backing unified behind the New-Deal control. Unity of attitude and clarity of aim have not characterized our major parties, yet without such a foundation presidential responsibility must remain tenuous. Wherein has our party system failed? It has not provided the president with dependable national support. But our Constitution is equally at fault in this regard, if fault it be.

Our party system is appropriate to our governmental structure. The one cannot be radically altered without change in the other. A meaningful and responsible national party committed to a definite legislative program cannot be reconciled with fixed periodic elections, staggered at different intervals, for Senate, president, and House. Nor does judicial review harmonize with such a view of presidential responsibility.

The actual operation of our system compels the conclusion that our parties have not been agencies upon which the president can rely for the realization of his policies. Party loyalties are useful in organizing the houses of Congress and in managing procedure; but the articulation of executive and administrative branches in the creative formulation of public policy cannot be embraced by the meager manipulative powers of party leaders.

Party control, if it is to be persistently effective, must be based upon a unity of interests and ideas. Lacking this, party loyalty is largely a product of sentiment, tradition, and convenience. Manipulation rather than discipline, and negotiation rather than authority, determine party behavior. If party leadership were to be made effective, party leaders would have to be allowed a hand in the nomination of candidates and the management of campaigns. Lacking the sanctions that ensue from such participation, the party leaders in Congress must rely almost wholly upon control of procedure. Even here disagreement among the leaders themselves may at times vitiate their power. The party as a link between legislative and executive branches provides a very uncertain connection except at those times when the chief executive is sustained by widespread public support. Under the best of conditions the party tie is a weak link; often it is a missing one.

The price of coherent effective party leadership is obedience and loyalty on the part of the rank and file to their leaders. Such loyalty may at times look like subservience.

On the other hand, the absence of party control may mean the negation of leadership and responsibility. Under a parliamentary system, M.P.'s are expected to follow the lead of their party chieftains. On the other hand, as Lord Bryce has said, "In America no candidate pledges himself to support a particular Congressional leadership. It would be thought unbecoming in him to do so."[2] The candidate must stand on his own feet. He may at times benefit by the popular enthusiasm for the presidential candidate of his party, but he must fight his political battles in his own locality with relatively little assistance from national headquarters. Most congressmen are still independent political entrepreneurs, seeking power in various areas and not beholden to a national party machine. The congressman has an ever-growing importance in seeking to redress grievances and to check abuses by the bureaucracy. The elective official must think of voters as individuals. He cannot depend for support upon a strong national party organization. The precarious position of our elected representatives, with all its disadvantages, keeps these politicians attentive to the desires and sentiments of the average man as no other system can.

Congress is composed of politicians whose political lives depend upon the loyalty of one Congressional district or, in the case of senators, upon a single state. This fact conditions the whole problem of party control of Congress. There are, moreover, divergences between left and right wings of each party which make unity of purpose difficult to achieve. The existence of the two houses, furthermore, means a jealous guarding of prerogatives. Sometimes grave disagreements occur between House and Senate, with little reference to

[2]James Bryce, *The American Commonwealth*. (New York: The Macmillan Company, 1910) 165.

partisan issues. For instance, administration leaders suggested in a recent session that the House Ways and Means Committee hold joint sessions with the Senate Finance Committee. The proposal was coldly rejected. "Let the other House hold its hearings," each side declared. This attitude means a duplication of testimony and a waste of time and energy. More important, however, from the point of view of responsible legislators, are the mutual belligerency and unwillingness to co-operate that are constantly apparent.

Our legislatures have long been held in distrust. The deflation of the legislature has been under way for many years, beginning in the seventies, with the disgust that followed the disclosures of venality among legislators. A deeper and more persistent cause was the belief that the power of the people must be expressed more directly. State constitutions became more detailed; provisions were made for popular lawmaking through the initiative and referendum. Our representative assemblies were said to be dominated by special interests; the voice of the people must speak for itself or through the popularly elected chief executive. This official, it was hoped, would protect the people from the selfish interests controlling the representative assemblies. There were doubtless good reasons for a shift in emphasis from corrupt or poorly managed legislative bodies to more responsible and perhaps more honest executive leadership. In any event accountability was easier. Grievances could be heaped on the head of one symbolic figure. And later the rascal could be driven from office.

A fact overlooked and still generally disregarded is that a transfer of power from the legislative to the executive branch does not eliminate the drives of special interests: it only forces them to seek different channels. Their demands and their bargaining are no longer plainly visible tactics. Instead of getting legislators to do their logrolling on the floor of the assembly, special interest representatives and administrators do their bargaining in the privacy of their own offices. This may have certain advantages. Decisions can be made with more attention to the details of the case, the needs of those affected, and the problems of administration involved. The parties at interest do not feel required to talk to the galleries: they can talk to the point. To this extent the "public interest" may be better served; but so far as substance is concerned, both sides must deal with particular concrete interests. Their objective must be the satisfactory adjustment of these conflicts. While they may lay the groundwork the final onus of decision falls to the legislator.

Congress is often its own worst enemy. Legislators fear to grant wide discretionary powers to the executive branch, particularly in the case of relief appropriations, and yet conscientious Congressional leaders fear even more the consequences of throwing such legislation into the pork barrel.

In calling attention to the weaknesses in the operation of our system let us not conclude that factionalism means anarchy, or a lack of discipline an absence of co-operation. Our institutions must be judged by their products. Congress and the president, despite dramatic difficulties, nevertheless have advanced in recent years the borders of public policy to meet needs long overdue and now accepted by both parties. Moreover when the need was clear Congress demonstrated that it could act despite partisan rivalries.

On the majority of issues the party takes no stand. There is no more scholarly observer than Congressman Luce, who states, "The machine rarely controls more than a part of the members of a party. The machine meddles very little with general legislation."[3] Since all members can introduce any bills they please, the party could hardly take any stand upon this great deluge of proposals. Moreover, many committees of Congress are habitually nonpartisan in their consideration of legislative proposals. Congress can fulfill a useful purpose as an outlet for opinion, as a vantage point for appeals to the voter and attacks or eulogies on the administration. With one-third of the Senate coming up for re-election every two years, and the entire House at the same interval, there operates in Congress a constant readjustment to the temper of public opinion. Congress is supposed to be a representative assembly. This it is, but it represents more effectively the stable constituencies than those which shift their political loyalties periodically. The whole apparatus of party controls within Congress tends to place power in the hands of the party veterans. This is but another way of strengthening localism and cannot result in responsible party control. It is a rule by a coterie which is in turn the fortuitous product of isolated local situations. Political machines may elect a congressman year after year; the longer his service, the greater are his chances for influence. There is no connection here with a program for which responsibility to a wider public is assumed.

The seniority rule, therefore, serves to insulate committee chairmen from direct responsibility to public opinion. Since promotion to committee positions of importance goes to those men having the longest span of continuous service, the most important positions in Congress fall to the congressmen from "regular districts." The legislators with the best chance of getting such appointments are those coming from states

[3]Luce, *op. cit.*, pp. 403, 504.

which are habitually Republican or Democratic. On the other hand, representatives of pivotal states, which swing from one party to the other, find it difficult or impossible to stay in office continuously for any considerable period of time.

Thus we habitually find in influential positions congressmen from traditionally loyal regions. They are much less aware of changing currents of opinion than are congressmen younger in service. The public attitude on any issue which may serve to bring the party into power does not, however, account for their own presence in the representative assembly. They would be there anyway.

This situation was strikingly demonstrated in the New Deal. In 1933 an administration came into power in response to a great public reaction against the policies of traditional Republicanism. The president preached a new doctrine. He depended for advice upon men new to public life. He gathered ideas from new sources, but in seeking to translate these ideas into law he was forced to rely upon old-line Democrats from traditional strongholds, whether in the Solid South, or in machine-bossed urban districts. During the crisis period these men were loyal to their party leader and were ready to follow his direction. But they were often confused and sometimes alarmed by the New Deal proposals. For example, Chairman Doughton of the House Ways and Means Committee, a man of sincerity, public spirit, and fidelity, was expected to direct his committee in their consideration of measures far outside his background, experience, and philosophy as a country banker and North Carolina farmer. Difficulties also arose from the fact that the powerful House Rules Committee was not wholly in sympathy with the New Deal.

Our system makes the newly elected president dependent upon veteran members of Congress for the consummation of his program. He has no authority to force action on their part. He can only hope for their co-operation. Yet the fact that they are influential in committees means that they come from those parts of the country least likely to reflect current political changes.

The seniority rule sometimes creates chairmen who are not even *persona grata* to the bulk of their own party. While they are more often party wheel horses, sometimes insurgents, called, on occasion, sons of wild jackasses, have reached chairmanships through seniority. Thus in the 72nd Congress insurgents headed three of the most important committees—Borah, Foreign Affairs; Norris, Judiciary; and Couzens, Interstate Commerce. During this same Congress the ultra-conservative Smoot was chairman of the Senate Finance Committee, and the conservative Jones was chairman of the Appropriations Committee. The seniority rule, by freeing men from fear of demotion, further frees them from control by the party.

To look to Congress for responsible control is to look to politicians, each dependent for his power upon holding his constituency. In some instances a single senator has been able to impose an enormous weight in affairs affecting the whole nation yet remain politically answerable to only a tiny segment. For example, Senator Borah built a great career for himself in obstruction and studied opposition; the influence of such a veteran on public affairs was far in excess of the importance of the state or interests that he represented. On the other hand, members reflecting the newest discontents of the voters are treated as neophytes.

If we go back to the time when Congress was organized

to maintain discipline among its members and hence act as a responsible body, we find power tightly held.

> This authority [writes George Rothwell Brown] was absorbed by the Speaker, and actually was exercised by a coterie of men, of long experience and sound training, and proved devotion to the party interest, who generally came into the control of the majority, and hence of the House, through intellectual ability and the impregnability of position conferred by long service.[4]

Today the feeling against strict procedural control is strong. The Senate has preferred to tolerate filibustering rather than resort to a closure rule. The House submits to rules limiting debate and governing procedure only because business could not otherwise be transacted; but resentment against such interference with the freedom of the members is always near the surface.

During the first New Deal Congress the Rules Committee held the House to the strictest limitations in discussing legislation. Special rules directed the consideration of all the important legislation of the session, and the emergency banking and economy acts were handled under even more extraordinary procedure. A sense of grievance among the members was voiced in complaints that the Rules Committee treated the membership without courtesy or consideration; that committees reported bills without critical deliberation; that members were expected to vote upon measures when no printed copies were available for study, and when even those sponsoring a measure could not adequately explain the terms of their bill; and that the leaders, when the House was or-

[4]From *The Leadership of Congress*, by George Rothwell Brown. Copyright 1922, p. 16. Used by special permission of the publishers, The Bobbs-Merrill Company.

ganized, had promised to give the membership an opportunity to participate in the direction of policy and had failed to do so. "Now," asserted one member, "we are nothing but rubbers stamps!" The experience of recent sessions with the discharge rule shows the internal struggle between the party leaders and factions among the rank and file.

One of the first acts of the Democrats when they gained control of the House in 1931 was immediately to liberalize the discharge rule and thereby force a bill from a committee for consideration on the floor, once a petition signed by 145 members was favorably voted upon. But when the Democratic leaders were themselves struggling to put through a legislative program in the first New Deal Congress they saw the need for stricter discipline.

Actual rebellion against tighter party control appeared when the leaders suggested abrogating the liberal discharge rule. Fifty-nine Democrats, including the leaders of the inflation and veterans' bonus blocs, held a rump caucus to protest against changing the rule. Party leaders were confident that they could secure enough votes to raise the required number of signatures on a discharge petition from 145 to 218. They could thus prevent a minority from bringing up for discussion issues which might be embarrassing to the administration. The protestors withdrew when they saw the determined disapproval of the leaders, who decided not to force the issue, although they had enough votes to change the rule. "As a matter of fact," said Speaker Rainey, "the minute anybody starts a discharge petition, we can have the committee bring in the bill with an adverse report, and that will end it." The appearance of harmony was restored within the party. It was more important to strive for agreement upon the pending legislation than to start a fight over rules.

By the second session of the 73rd Congress minority blocs had become more insistent. The struggle over rules of procedure was no sham battle but a grim fight between the administration forces seeking to carry through a program, and strong blocs alert to forward their own measures. If the House leaders had a broadsword in the gag rule, minorities had a dagger in the discharge rule. Their weapon was keen, though limited in range. Since its "reform" on December 8, 1931, the discharge rule had been used persistently for the benefit of special interests. During this session it was referred to as an "asinine rule," and its amendment was demanded in the name of "majority government." The floor leader and speaker attempted during the special session and also at the beginning of this session, to bring about a return to the old rule requiring 218 signatures on a discharge petition. The existing rule, declared Representative McDuffie, "is a millstone about the neck of the majority charged with the responsibility of legislation." On the other hand, its effectiveness in securing legislation had been slight. Nevertheless its use proved embarrassing to the House leaders on more than one occasion. In the 74th Congress the Democratic leaders decided that they had had enough of the liberal rule.

Immediately after the organization of the House, Representative O'Connor offered an amendment to the rule, requiring that henceforth a majority of the House must sign the petition before a vote could be entertained requiring a committee to report. The expected crocodile tears were shed by opponents, who evoked the shades of Patrick Henry and Samuel Adams in stigmatizing this "backward move to Cannonism." Republicans pointed out the embarrassing truth that the real purpose of the amendment was to increase the control of Democratic leaders over their own followers, since the 102 Republicans, even under the liberal discharge rule, could not even muster the 145 signatures required for a petition. Since the Democratic caucus had already agreed to the change by a vote of 225 to 60, the rules were altered by a House vote of 243 to 165. The basic reason for opposition to the change was thus frankly explained by one congressman: "If there is anything dear to the hearts of the organized groups of this country, organized labor, organized veterans, organized farmers, it is this vehicle for getting before the House legislation for consideration." The House leaders, however, were bent upon greasing the legislative machine for those measures dear to the heart of the chief executive.

If Congress were differently organized for handling its heavy responsibilities we would hear less about the need for increased executive control. This is not to suggest a return to Cannonism. It is rather to state the need for scrutiny of the seniority rule and the present internal organization of the House and Senate. Congress has the responsibility of clarifying its own problems of control. Much could be done toward emphasizing the general and national interest as against special and local pressures. The party caucus might be developed as a counterweight to the push of special privilege. Representatives holding a fresh mandate from the voters might be elected by caucus vote to positions of influence on committees.

The seniority rule is not to be interpreted, however, as an obstacle to responsible party government. It might more accurately be treated as a substitute. It practically eliminates the difficult decisions of power distribution which can so thoroughly disrupt human relations. The only alternatives to seniority would be a pure lottery or a strong party high command with sanctions potent enough to enforce its decisions. Yet we may have to pay a heavy price for the present undisciplined decentralized process. Party responsibility can only be erected on a strong national party organization that actively aids in local elections. The presidential policies of the New Deal, we are now discovering, never permeated the Democratic party as a whole. Conservative Democrats followed the president as a matter of expediency. The party as such has not stood responsible for all the New Deal policies. The seniority rule sidesteps the allotment of political influence in terms of considerations of policy.

Outwardly our system provides great freedom to congressmen in initiating legislation. They do not have to submit to a lottery such as that imposed upon members of Parliament, who must depend upon good fortune for an opportunity to introduce a private member's bill.

Bills introduced in Congress are referred to the appropriate committee, there to be pigeonholed or reported out favorably or unfavorably. Since bills are introduced so freely, the great majority must die in committee and even those surviving must next win the favor of the Rules Committee if they are to be adequately considered on the floor of the House. The Rules Committee, although supposedly designed for the conduct of orderly business, has in fact been influenced at times more by the substantive nature of the bill than by its relative importance. Thus even important bills sponsored by the president but embodying policy distasteful to members of the Rules Committee have on occasion had difficulty in reaching the floor of the House.

The struggle over the holding company legislation shows the type of guerilla warfare that can be fought so persistently against even a major administrative objective.

To a particular degree, the president made the holding company legislation his own concern. In messages to Congress on January 4, March 12, and June 19, 1935, he referred directly to the abolition of unnecessary holding companies. This became the major issue over which the regulation of interstate electrical power sale and transmission was fought. Where a bill encounters the strong opposition of a powerful lobby, the legislative process discloses the difficulties that arise from divided responsibility and separate authorities. There is little "drive" in the system. Shilly-shally is reinforced by dilly-dally. Such procedure was doubtless intended to limit an arbitrary executive, to curb the impulse of "popular passion," or to bring about a compromise of sectional differences. Present-day demands, however, mean that the federal government is more often concerned with curbing the force of some powerful economic or social group outside the official structure than with maintaining a balance among the political forces represented in the various branches of the government. The bonds of party are hardly strong enough to contrive a united resistance to the organized drive of a powerful economic group. The course of the holding company legislation illustrates these observations and serves as an example of the problems of executive-legislative relations.

On behalf of the administration, one bill rigidly regulating holding companies was introduced in both houses in February, 1935. More than three months later, on May 14, the Senate reported out a modified version of the bill. The extent and nature of the changes made by the Interstate Commerce Committee were not apparent, however, because while the committee considered S. 1725, they reported back a new bill, S. 2796. The original bill, plus the committee amendments, was presented as a new bill. The procedure was criticized on the ground that "senators will be placed in an embarrassing position by having presented to them a bill without being able to ascertain, from an examination of the bill itself, what particular amendments have been adopted by the committee." On the floor of the Senate, attention centered on Section 11. Senator Dieterich, a Democrat, introduced an amendment modifying this section, but administration spokesmen said that his proposal would take out "the heart of the bill." Senator Wheeler drew the issue squarely between following Dieterich and following Roosevelt. He read a private letter from the president as evidence of White House opposition to any amendments that struck at Section 11. By a vote of 45 to 44, Dieterich's amendment was defeated on June 11. This vote cut directly across party lines, the Democrats dividing 29 yea to 35 nay, the Republicans 15 yea to 8 nay. The votes of the Farmer-Laborite Shipstead and the Progressive La Follette saved the administration. The core of the opposition came from the New England and Atlantic seaboard states. The East North Central states were about evenly divided. The support for the president came from the South and the West, the Mountain and Pacific areas being overwhelmingly opposed to the proposal of the Democratic Dieterich of Illinois. A second test was immediately precipitated by Lonergan, Democratic senator from Connecticut. His modifying amendment was voted down by 45 to 43. The line-up remained the same, except that the Democratic Ashurst of Arizona refrained from voting. The holding company bill passed the Senate by 56 to 32.

In the House the bill encountered greater difficulties. After protracted consideration, the Committee on Interstate and Foreign Commerce, by a vote of 15 to 7, reported the measure on June 22 without the "death sentence." "Fifteen Democrats," a member of the committee stated, "and one Republican on the committee voted for the bill. One Democrat voted 'present.' Six Republicans voted in the opposition." The strategy in the House turned upon the substitution of the Senate "death sentence" provision. By a teller vote, this proposal was voted down on July 1 by 146 to 216. A record vote on July 2 showed that the House, by 258 to 147, preferred its own bill to that of the Senate. A sectional analysis of this vote reveals that the delegations from the populous industrial states on the Atlantic seaboard and north of the Ohio River were overwhelmingly opposed to a drastic holding company policy. The great majority of congressmen from these states that control the greatest proportion of electoral votes were unwilling to go along with the president. The Democrats split, 166 to 130. The Middle Atlantic states voted by 67 to 13, the South Atlantic states by 42 to 8, and the East North Central states by 56 to 27, to support the House bill. The delegations from the regions most consistent in their support of the president were divided in their votes on the holding company measure. The bill finally passed the House by 323 to 81 after a motion to send it back to committee with instruction to eliminate the House "death sentence" had failed by 93 to 312.

The two houses were thus deadlocked; nor was the conference committee able to reach an agreement. When the time came to instruct the conferees of the House, another opportunity for a record vote was offered. By 210 to 155, the House refused to have its committee accept the Senate death-sentence proposal. Not until the Senate offered a compromise backed by the pleas of the party leaders would the House shift its position. The speaker entered the debate with an appeal directly to his fellow partisans to compromise the issue. Chairman Rayburn read a similar plea from the president. Fifty-nine Democrats changed their minds (as of August 1), and the bill was passed by 219 to 142. Both houses accepted the conference report on August 24. The president won, but only after a prolonged struggle.

This one example drawn from the legislative process shows how freely party lines are overriden by sectional interests and how our present system provides no means sufficiently strong for party or executive control. Such controls are suspect and we apparently have been willing to pay the necessary price of confusion in order to retain the present procedures.

Our parties are divided internally. As already noted, the seniority rule has a tendency to bring to influential committee posts members of the more conservative faction. Party leaders by virtue of their position are also expected to act as presidential spokesmen when a fellow partisan is in the White House. Yet the chairman of important committees have refused at times to support the party policies sponsored by the president.

The only contribution that partisanship as such can make in the problem of bridging the gap between the White House and Congress lies in the control of procedures. This in practice is dependent upon the personal relationship existing between the chief executive and party leaders. Party leaders may or may not turn Congressional procedures to forward presidential aims. In other words, the president has no effective channel of communication to his party in Congress. He must work through Congressional leaders or negotiate with individuals: he cannot deal with his fellow partisans as a group.

If a clear party program is to be passed by Congress, then the compromise that now takes place in committees must be transplanted to the party caucus and private conferences among party leaders. But merely bringing party members together by no means guarantees agreement, and party leaders realize that the caucus may get out of hand. Such rebelliousness stresses the tenuous hold that the leaders have on their fellow partisans. Political rivalries within the party ranks may be as keen as those dividing the parties.

In recent years the party caucus has not served as a significant device for procuring a united party front. Each house holds caucuses for bringing together the members who belong to the same party in order to determine how their respective houses shall be organized. The caucus is seldom convened after problems of organization are settled. When outside pressures threaten to disrupt the administrative program, a caucus may be called in order to rally party support and establish a united front. It serves to restore the confidence of partisans in their fellows. United they can withstand the demands of special interests; divided, they may fall victims to the lobbyist.

An examination of the process of lawmaking during early New Deal Congresses emphasizes the fact that despite the emergency conditions necessitating quick and decisive action, and despite the unified support given the president by the general public, factions persisted in Congress. The farm bloc, the veterans' bloc, the inflationist bloc, and others gained strength because of the critical economic situation and threatened at times to obstruct the president's program. Party solidarity was uncertain, and party control was limited in its powers.

The table on the following page indicates the promptness with which the first session of the 73rd Congress acted upon the president's proposals.

The proved capacity of our system to operate rapidly and powerfully when emergency demands, must not be overlooked simply because the Congress and the president squabble openly in normal times. The whole issue is dramatically posed in the following interchange found in recent hearings on proposed wartime profiteering legislation.

SENATOR LEE: General, can you really prosecute a war with all the vigor of the Nation unless the Nation in a sense resolves itself into a complete dictatorship, giving the Commander in Chief power over everything in the Nation?

GENERAL JOHNSON: There is an element of truth in that, but I think you can go too far with all that. I don't think Congress should adjourn on the beginning of war. I think they have to support the President. I will tell you this, that if ever a war comes where popular sentiment as reflected in Congress does not support the war and does not support the President, there ain't going to be no war. You cannot wage a war with this country any more which is not . . . a popular war . . . In the Civil War we tried to put over conscription in this country. The country was divided and the war sentiment was not complete even in the North. It was an absolute and utter failure. When the World War came on, . . . I proposed that the draft be executed as it was executed, which was practically to place the control in the local communities, and almost everybody said that was crazy. Mr. Baker finally decided that was the way, and what he said was this: "If the local

Number of Bill	Title	Proposed by President	Passed House	Passed Senate	Date Approved	No. of Law or Resolution	Hours of General Debate in House
H. R. 1491	Emergency banking relief	Mar. 9	Mar. 9	Mar. 9	Mar. 9	1	40 min.
H. R. 2820	Maintenance of government's credit (economy bill)	Mar. 10	Mar. 11	Mar. 15	Mar. 20	2	2
H. R. 3341	Permit and tax beer	Mar. 13	Mar. 14	Mar. 16	Mar. 22	3	3
H. R. 3835	Emergency agricultural relief; farm mortgage; currency issuance and regulation	Mar. 16	Mar. 22	Apr. 28	May 12	10	5²
S. 598	Unemployment relief (reforestation)	Mar. 21	Mar. 29	Mar. 28	Mar. 31	5	5
H. R. 4606	Federal emergency relief	Mar. 21	Apr. 21	May 1	May 12	15	2
H. R. 5980	Supervision of traffic in securities	Mar. 29	May 5	May 8	May 27	22	5
H. R. 5081	Muscle Shoals and Tennessee Valley Authority	Apr. 10	Apr. 25	May 3	May 18	17	6
H. R. 5240	Relief of small home owners	Apr. 13	Apr. 28	June 5	June 13	43	1½
S. 1580	Railroad reorganization and relief	May 4	June 5	May 27	June 16	68	3
H. R. 5755	Industrial recovery; public construction and taxation	May 17	May 26	June 9	June 16	67	6

communities are not in favor of this war we had better not go into it," which was another way of expressing the thought I have just tried to express.

I do not think that the idea of putting the power in the President and everybody else abdicating is necessary for the purpose of war on the theory that there will be a division in Congress to the extent that will paralyze the Nation at war. I think if you have not got Congress behind the war, you will not have a war anyway.[5]

In times of emergency Congress is capable of swift action. If Congressional behavior discloses pettiness and self-seeking, it is well to recall that Congress is a representative assembly. Congress has also exhibited nobler traits when occasions demand. When popular government seems threatened from abroad surely the first step for its protection is not the abrogation of Congressional powers. Congress is supposed to represent the voters, and if our assembly does not work with the chief executive, the battle for democracy is lost before a shot is fired. The problem is to insure the representative character of Congress. Here the danger to watch is the effect of the seniority rule and of blocs that use obstructionist procedures for selfish ends.

[5]Hearings on S. 25 before the Senate Committee on Military Affairs, 75th Congress, 1st Session, pp. 94–95.

Chapter III

Methods of Presidential Control

While popular confidence is at bottom the support upon which the chief executive must rely in dealing with Congress, in actual practice the president must use his wits and his skill in handling men if he would make his power effective. This is borne out by long experience, though it seems always rather shocking to those who envisage politics in more heroic terms. Many years ago Justice Story lamented:

"The Executive is compelled to resort to secret and unseen influences, to private interviews, and private arrangements, to accomplish its own appropriate purposes, instead of proposing and sustaining its own duties and measures by a bold and manly appeal to the nation in the face of its representatives."[1]

These views reflect a stiff-bosomed, frock-coated approach to politics that has not yet entirely disappeared. The statesman is still thought of as a dignified, unbending figure to whom tact is incompatible with integrity. Manly appeals to the nation have their place in executive-legislative relationships, but private interviews and private arrangements may

[1]Story on the Constitution, section 869 *et seq*. Quoted in Senate Report 837, February 4, 1881.

be much more important and indeed more worthy of respect than spectacular and heroic public stands for principle. Were it not for the constant resort to "private arrangements" our system would burst from sheer bombast.

One strength of our presidency is its great adaptability. There is as much variety in presidential relations with Congress as there are differences in the men occupying the White House. Despite the variation observable under different administrations, the president has clearly come to take a more active part in the legislative process. In this regard the testimony of a direct witness of presidential routine is pertinent. Ike Hoover spent forty-two years around the White House. He writes:

In the earlier years the Presidents made less noticeable effort to influence legislation. Harrison, Cleveland, and McKinley did not appear to those in the White House to do much along this line. Roosevelt seemed to be the one who started the custom as it is carried on today. Yet he was more formal about it, arranging to discuss the general aspect of a question some time in advance.

Taft continued in this practice, though apparently with less success. Especially was this noticeable in the making of the tariff bill passed during his Administration.

Wilson did less to influence Congress than either of his two predecessors. His method was to resort to the telephone rather than to send for the members of the Senate and House to come to him. He felt it to be a delicate proposition and, after making his suggestions, hardly ever conferred with the members while a bill was being debated. He seemed to feel that he had expressed his opinion and there was no further argument. At times a party leader would tell him of plans to change a measure under consideration, whereupon he would call up a Senator or a member of the House and tell him very sharply and in a few words that no change was admissible. This generally brought about the desired results.

President Harding's methods were so varied that they are difficult to explain. He was on close terms with a great number of Senators and Congressmen and discussed official business with them on all occasions. Meals, golf, card games, travels, walks, every place was a field of action. They argued with him as they have done with no other President and generally had their way, convincing him that whatever they did was right. He never seemed to be concerned with the fate of a measure under consideration, depending more on these so-called friends to take care of his interests.

President Coolidge was different from all the rest. He seemed always to be watching, rather suspicious lest something be "put over" on him. He certainly kept good track of what was going on at the Capitol. He was continually sending for Congressmen to confer with them about pending legislation. He would read in the morning papers of plans for legislation and immediately have word telephoned to the Senator or Representative chiefly concerned to stop in at the Executive Offices on his way to the Capitol. This was almost a daily occurrence.[2]

One of the most curious of Coolidge's tactics was the White House breakfast. The newspapers made much of the president's meeting with political leaders over sausages and griddle cakes. Actually little deliberative discussion seems to have taken place; the breakfasts were a social gesture,

[2] Irwin Hood Hoover, *Forty-two Years in the White House.* (Boston: Houghton Mifflin Company, 1934) 250–52.

well intentioned but rather inept. Apparently "statesmen," like humbler breeds of men, care little about breakfast sociability. Excuses were often offered. There were no important discussions around the table to attract the guests. "They seemed always to enjoy the food," Ike Hoover concludes, "bacon and eggs, sausage and cakes, fruit, toast and coffee— but they never seemed to understand the idea of having them there either for social purposes, of which they saw no evidence, or for official matters, of which they heard nothing. It was just a breakfast!"[3]

Each man to his taste. The record of Congressional disagreement with Coolidge's policies shows many major defeats for him. He may have fed his guests sausages; he often had to "eat crow" himself. The soldiers' bonus was passed over his veto; he favored adherence to the World Court, but the Senate would not concur; he opposed Japanese exclusion, but Congress tacked it to an immigration bill. On taxation, on economy, and on agricultural policy Congress ran counter to the president's desires.[4]

Presidential ingenuity has hit upon numerous other ways of dealing with Congress. Woodrow Wilson revived an early practice by delivering his messages to Congress in person. Less well remembered is the fact that toward the beginning of his first term he frequently made use of the president's room near the Senate chamber in order to be at hand for frequent conferences with influential senators. The most general method, of course, remained the "private

[3]*Ibid.*, p. 128.

[4]From *The Powers of the President: Problems of American Democracy*, by W. E. Binkley, p. 248–49. Copyright 1937, by Doubleday, Doran and Company, Inc.

interviews and private arrangements" scorned by Justice Story.

Speaker Cannon has left a graphic picture of his personal relations with President Theodore Roosevelt:

After I became Speaker of the House, my conferences with President Roosevelt were frequent, two or three times a week when Congress was in session, and sometimes daily. The President would write a note asking me to stop on my way to the capitol, or his secretary would telephone a similar message to my house. My calls were so frequent they excited comment and may have created the belief in the "influence" I exercised over the President; but almost invariably I called at his request and did not seek an appointment. There were reports in the newspapers of friction between us, which Roosevelt took notice of on one occasion by writing me: "I care not a rap about the reports of clashes and the predictions of clashes between you and me. We can handle that matter ourselves. Come up some evening for a long talk, Tuesday or Wednesday or Thursday evening about 9:30, if you can, so that we shall be free from interruption, and let me know when to expect you."

Usually, we found it more convenient to meet in the evening, especially when we wanted to be undisturbed, and it was then, sitting about the fire or later in his study, we talked things over until midnight. We did not always talk shop . . . We did not always agree; in fact, we more often disagreed, but seldom in principle and usually as to practical methods. Roosevelt had the outlook of the Executive and the ambition to do things; I had the more confined outlook of the legislator who had to consider ways of meeting the expenditures of new departures and expansions in Government. These talks were seldom official. They were more the presentation of two schools of government by two men who recognized there were two sides to every question and who had opposing theories.[5]

This rather idyllic picture of two thoughtful, friendly statesmen seated by the hearth in the White House was not to last. Roosevelt saw the gulf widen between himself and the conservative leaders in Congress. Aldrich and Hale, as well as Cannon, held to views with which the president found agreement increasingly difficult.

I made a resolute effort to get on with all three and with their followers [he stated], and I have no question that they made an equally resolute effort to get on with me. We succeeded in working together, although with increasing friction, for some years, I pushing forward and they hanging back. Gradually, however, I was forced to abandon the effort to persuade them to come my way, and then I achieved results only by appealing over the heads of the Senate and House leaders to the people, who were the masters of both of us.[6]

By the end of his second term Roosevelt was fighting with the Republican majorities in the two houses as bitterly "as if they and I had belonged to opposite political parties." The course of Woodrow Wilson's clash with Congress toward the end of his administration followed through to tragic futility.

Our presidents cannot afford the luxury of fighting with Congress. The political life of our chief executive is so short and his effectiveness is so dependent upon Congressional

[5]L. White Busbey, *Uncle Joe Cannon.* (New York: Henry Holt and Company, 1927) 216.

[6]Theodore Roosevelt, *Theodore Roosevelt: An Autobiography.* (New York: The Macmillan Company, 1913) 383–84.

support that a protracted battle, even though successful, is a Pyrrhic victory at best. Presidential relations with Congress have so often run a course, from friendly consultation at the outset to bitter recrimination at the end, that the pattern has almost become standardized.

The Hoover administration followed the familiar sequence of repudiation at the end. James E. Watson relates that he had a private telephone connection with the White House. "When I became leader, he [Hoover] had this wire put in so that we might talk to each other freely without any interference day or night."[7] He also conferred with the president regularly: "As leader in the Senate, I had breakfast with the president at least once a week, generally twice, to discuss legislative matters, and on those occasions he was always very courteous and affable and willing to listen to my advice on legislative matters in the Senate. . . ."[8] By the end of Hoover's administration his relations with Congress were at a very low ebb. Congress was divided in control.

Roosevelt, when taking over in March, 1933, is commonly depicted as holding an easy ascendancy over Congress. Certainly the legislature was unusually docile. Yet even in this time of extremity party discipline was not readily accepted; the impetus for agreement was effectively exerted not because of party control so much as through the weight of a public demand for action. A detailed examination of those critical days of the New Deal is well worth recalling.

That the president was prepared, if necessary, to upset the "normal balance of executive and legislative authority" he made clear in his inaugural address. The chief executive

[7]From *As I Knew Them* by James E. Watson. Copyright 1936, p. 276. Used by special permission of the publishers, The Bobbs-Merrill Company.

[8]*Ibid.*, p. 262.

became the chief lawmaker. He applied to Congress the "discipline and direction under leadership" that he saw demanded in the popular mandate of his election. Protests against the assumption of dictatorial powers were overridden by the necessity of "broad executive power" for meeting emergency conditions. The oft-reiterated challenge of unconstitutionality the president had sought to forestall when he said on assuming office: "Our Constitution is so simple and practical that it is possible always to meet extraordinary needs by changes in emphasis and arrangement without loss of essential form." As the session proceeded, many so-called "essential forms" became essentially empty formalities. The president had become a prime minister.

To the public's demand for action, and the president's readiness to lead Congress, must be added that factor necessary for success—a majority party support in both houses. A common party label was no guarantee of unquestioning loyalty from the rank and file, but it did give the president control of the party organization. He was thus able in large measure to direct the deliberations of Congress. This was no small power as exercised by Franklin D. Roosevelt. He displayed remarkable skill in manipulating the attention of Congress and of the public. His messages to Congress were strategically timed and positive and specific in character. Disagreement with his proposals was interpreted by the general public as obstructionism. His swift pace, his boldness in assuming responsibility, and his definite recommendations not only stimulated popular support of his policy but at the same time branded as dissenters and critics congressmen holding to different policies. His radio talks to the nation served the double purpose of reassuring the people and breaking down resistance in Congress. Legislators were made only too well aware of the temper of their constituents.

Congressmen of both parties were willing to follow President Roosevelt's lead, and he managed his Congressional relations with great tact. Of course the pressure of the emergency and the solid public support behind the president must be understood as modifying normal relations, but even when this is allowed for, a full weight of political sagacity remains to account for his extraordinary success with Congress. The attitude of the Republicans was indicated when, following a caucus meeting, Floor Leader Snell declared: "Our policy will be to stand squarely behind the Democratic Administration in support of legislation to better conditions." At the end of the session, the president was able to thank both houses for a "spirit of teamwork" between the legislative and executive branches that in most cases "transcended party lines" and made possible "more wholehearted co-operation" than had been witnessed in "many a long year."

At the outset the organization of the House of Representatives in the 73rd Congress was the result of a "trade" among rival aspirants for office. Before the caucus met an "understanding" had been arranged among the several candidates for the speakership. Party positions of strategic importance were distributed among leaders from pivotal states. Support from the Ohio and New York delegations helped elect as speaker the first northern Democrat in over fifty years. Could the nation-wide Democratic strength be consolidated in the organization of the House? If the huge Democratic majority of 191 was to prove effective, harmony was necessary. Yet the presence of over 150 new members, bringing novel proposals for national salvation and knowing little of legislative problems, complicated the situation. The critical economic conditions made it essential that the House be organized for prompt and united action and that it respond to the leaders. The caucus helped to answer this need. It was useful in canvassing opinions, but the wide numerical margin of the majority party made severe regimentation avoidable in many individual cases.

The creation of a Democratic steering committee was forecast by the election of Speaker Rainey. His advocacy of this committee was considered a leading factor in his selection as speaker, particularly in view of the large number of Democrats coming from states previously Republican. The House was organized on an entirely new basis, in the opinion of the new speaker. The object of this innovation was to keep the party together and to ascertain the degree of party support for the Democratic program. "It is a long step forward," Rainey declared, "and it takes from the speaker power he has arbitrarily exercised and gives it back to the House. Failures in the last Congress have been due to the fact that the determination of policies has come entirely from the speaker's chair; it will now come from the party. We will put over Mr. Roosevelt's program."

Unwittingly, the speaker seemed to touch the significant factor in the scheme of Democratic organization. The possible contradiction of party policies and presidential program was resolved by the speaker's easy identification of the two. Independent party leadership among the House Democrats was rendered well-nigh impossible by the plan of party organization. Responsibility for control was lost in the search for harmony. The president stood clear of this intertwining confusion of party agencies. The system was well adapted to carrying out his commands, but poorly devised for independent control by the party officials in the legislature.

The steering committee was composed of one representative each for the fifteen districts into which the country was divided. As ex-officio members were added the speaker, the whip, the majority floor leader, and the chairman of the caucus. The delegations from a given district elected one of their number to represent them on the steering committee. Since the speaker had sponsored the establishment of this committee, he could not very well ignore its existence or attempt to override it. Yet coherent steering could not be attempted with nineteen pilots at the helm.

That the party organization was better designed for carrying out orders from above than for initiating policies was emphasized by the increased importance of the whips. Especially did the new members need direction and advice. Chief Whip Greenwood accordingly named assistant whips for the regional divisions identical with the steering committee districts. These lieutenants were liaison officers between the party officials and the Democratic delegations from the states in their district. Each whip was answerable for the members of the party from his region. The chief whip consulted regularly with the speaker and the floor leader and met with the steering committee; he instructed his assistants at weekly conferences. The whip characterized his task as one of "benevolent persuasion." The great party majority permitted him on occasion to relax discipline where a congressman had made prior commitments. Here was a systematic arrangement for passing along orders, for checking votes and attendance, and for canvassing the opinions of the members.

The Democrats thus developed in this Congress an elaborate structure for party control, but placed no one at the top. The greater the number of separate agencies set up, the less likely was unified and responsible action, since no principle of hierarchy established a definite relationship of subordination to leadership. Members attempted to commit the party by working through the caucus. The steering committee, ostensibly representative, was an intermediary between caucus and leaders. Symbolizing a transfer of powers from the speaker to the members, the committee was not properly composed for executive action. Its functions became "advisory." Those holding the titular positions of command in the party organization attained to office by a close trade rather than a clear victory. They exhibited their power through control of legislative procedure rather than through their influence over their fellows.

Party control in this Congress must be discussed in terms of presidential leadership. It was well that the president's wishes and the party program were regarded as identical in the minds of Rainey and his confreres. Presidential authority to dictate policy was unquestioned, and the machinery for aligning the members behind his measures fortunately was at hand; but the real nature of his control can only be understood by a close examination of Congressional relations.

The critical tension of the banking crisis made it imperative at the very first meeting of the new Congress that the president's guidance be accepted without hesitation. Majority Floor Leader Byrns, requesting "unanimous consent," introduced the emergency banking act with debate limited to forty minutes. In appealing for Republican support, Minority Floor Leader Snell stated: "The house is burning down, and the President of the United States says this is the way to put out the fire." The House had not yet adopted rules of procedure; the bill was not available in printed form; the members were acquainted with its contents by the reading clerk. But leaders of the House and Senate had met with the president the night before and had promised to expedite the measure. The bill passed the House without a record vote, received the approval of the Senate a few hours later, and was promulgated by the chief executive the same evening.

The next morning, March 10, the House received the president's message requesting authority for making drastic economies by cuts in the salaries of government employees and in the compensation of ex-service men. "For three long years the federal government has been on the road toward bankruptcy," the president stated. "For the fiscal year 1934, based on the appropriation bills passed by the last Congress and the estimated revenues, the deficit will probably exceed $1,000,000,000 unless immediate action is taken." On proposal of the majority floor leader, a special economy committee was created to act upon the president's message for the sake of "quick action" and to avoid waiting until the formation of the standing committees. The reports of this committee were given privileged status, and its jurisdiction was limited to the president's economy proposals.

But the Democratic rank and file likewise wished to discuss fiscal policy. "I wish respectfully to suggest to our leader," said Representative Woodrum, " . . . that he take the whole matter of the President's message into our family caucus and let us very frankly and freely consider it and discuss it." The caucus met the next morning and trouble began. The leaders were divided among themselves. Speaker Rainey was unable to align two-thirds of the members behind the president's economy bill, and it was with difficulty that the caucus was kept from agreeing to support the Browning amendment, a measure designed to emasculate the economy program. Immediately following this heated caucus, which ended in discord, the measure came before the House.

Despite the rebellious faction within their party, the leaders desired to pass the bill at once. In the caucus they had only their influence, but in the House they had more effective weapons. There, strong psychological conditions were in their favor, and a different atmosphere prevailed. Democrats who had viewed the bill unfavorably in secret caucus changed their point of view in the open debate, and the Democratic leaders found their hands strengthened by Republican support and by public approbation of the administration's position. "When the *Congressional Record* goes to President Roosevelt's desk in the morning," one of them asserted, "he will look over the roll call we are about to take, and I warn you new Democrats to be careful where your names are found." Hisses and groans greeted this admonition, but the point struck home.

The party leaders had a more tangible weapon in their control over procedure, and they used it with great skill. A special rule for bringing up the economy measure was inexpedient because such a rule must "lie over" a day unless passed by a two-thirds vote, and such a majority was lacking. The House parliamentarian advised the leaders that the desired immediate action could be had, strangely enough, by simply following the "regular order." This was possible since the calendars were clear, no standing committees had been appointed, and there was no business before the House wherewith obstructionists could effectively delay action. This procedure was a masterpiece of simplicity and directness without precedent in Congress in many years. After the opening prayer and approval of the minutes, the House proceeded at once to the orders of the day. The floor leader introduced a resolution providing that debate on the economy bill be limited to two hours and ruling out amendments. It was hoped that the amendment that had disrupted the caucus could thus be kept out of the House, but Representative Browning proved too experienced a parliamentarian to be thrust aside so easily. He saw that even under the resolution it would be in order for an opponent of the bill to offer a motion to recommit the bill to committee. An opening for amending the measure appeared in possible instructions to this committee. It was up to the Democratic leaders to forestall Representative Browning. How could the leader of the proveteran rebels be prevented from crippling the economy bill by his limiting amendment? A loophole was seen in a motion sponsored by Representative Connery of Massachusetts. This champion of the veterans wished to kill the economy bill entirely by returning it to committee without instructions. The leaders grasped this slender chance, for Connery's motion made possible a vote to recommit *without any modifying amendment.* The speaker used his right to recognize with decisive effect. Connery was called upon, Browning ignored. When the latter insisted that his amendment deserved recognition "after what occurred in the caucus this morning," the speaker coldly rejoined that the House had no knowledge of the caucus.

Many others were likewise willing to forget that disrupted party meeting. The Connery motion was defeated (ayes 90, noes 272) as the leaders had anticipated, and a roll call was at once requested on the bill, despite a roar of Democratic protest. The measure was passed by 266 (Dem. 197, Rep. 69) to 138 (Dem. 92, Rep. 41, F.-L. 5). Among the Democrats voting against the bill were the assistant floor leader, two members of the steering committee, and four of the party whips. If the Republicans had not crossed the aisle to support the president, his bill would have faced defeat.

Despite support from the president, the public, and even the opposition party, the party leaders had to exercise all their ingenuity in parliamentary procedure to put their measure through. A special rule, the right of recognition, and a roll call of names helped to outmaneuver the veterans' bloc in the House and frustrate the demands of this special interest. Income tax payments, moreover, were just falling due, and the public desire for genuine economies in government was evident. On Sunday, March 12, the president made an effective appeal to the nation over the radio, and Congress was held under close scrutiny.

When the economy bill was reported to the upper house on Monday, after a bitter struggle in the Finance Committee, senators took the opportunity to make general acknowledgments of letters too numerous to be handled by their clerical forces. "Bear in mind that the vast army comprising the unorganized majority is thoroughly aroused over reckless government expenditures and will not tolerate submission to organized minority groups." This quotation from one such message reflected the tenor of many others.

The American Legion did not give up the fight, but offered to accept a flat 25 per cent reduction in veterans' compensation. Senate leaders saw in this proposal an attempt to revive the Browning amendment and force a compromise. They were aware that the propaganda mills were grinding as the telegrams poured into their offices. As a protection from this lobbying, some senators insisted upon being bound to support the bill by a caucus vote. But the caucus, while endorsing the bill, declined to be bound against amendments. This gave the obstructionists their chance, and a long debate resulted. The opposition came not from the Republican leaders, but from a bloc, and the delay was vigorously deplored in view of the critical state of the government's finances. The granting of dictatorial powers to the president was defended on the ground that "Congress had abdicated its functions by its failure to act." The worst political crime of the time was inaction.

The president saw this and skillfully used it as a lever to move Congress. The very day on which the Senate was to consider the economy bill, he sent his brief, dramatic message recommending immediate modification of the Volstead Act. The public demand for economy was excelled only by its thirst for beer. The pressure upon the Senate for early action was more than that dilatory body could withstand. Two days after its introduction, the economy bill was passed, and on the day following beer was legalized.

The House, torn by the party disagreement over the vetterans' reductions, came together behind the terse beer message so clearly based upon the Democratic platform pledge. The president displayed his shrewd political sense by uniting his party at once upon this popular measure. House leaders were planning to adjourn and await the Senate's action on the economy bill when a telephone call from the White House apprised Speaker Rainey of the president's message. The air was cleared and the congressmen voted with alacrity.

The details of this legislative situation are worthy of close attention as an illustration of the enormous importance of skill in manipulation and timing and of the tactical value of procedural controls.

The leadership of Congress during the first New Deal session of Congress was sustained in large measure through the impetus to action engendered by the economic crisis. But weaknesses in the Congressional structure, hidden by the unifying effect of the emergency period, appeared clearly during later sessions. If opinion polls were any indication, there was continued wide popular support behind the chief executive. Yet in the face of this general approbation the president displayed a willingness to compromise with his early Congresses that stands in contrast with the attitude taken later. It seems clear that during 1934–35 President Roosevelt's tactics were directed not merely toward enhancing his own popularity, but also toward fortifying the political positions of his Congressional supporters. He was apparently profiting by the experience of his wartime chief, Woodrow Wilson. If he was to continue to make the presidential system work, he had to guard against the hazard of greatly diminished support in later sessions of Congress.

At the opening of the second session of the 73rd Congress the president addressed both houses in friendly and intimate fashion. His was not a formal report on the state of the union, but a broad, even vague, statement of aspirations and a personal acknowledgment of Congressional co-operation. "Out of these friendly contacts," he said, "we are, fortunately, building a strong and permanent tie between the legislative and executive branches of the government. The letter of the Constitution wisely declared a separation, but the impulse of common purpose declares a union."

To cement and render workable this union was his constant endeavor. He showed a hesitancy to commit himself until the time was ripe for action, and he was willing to compromise in order to maintain cordial relations with Congress. He drove with a looser rein during this session and turned aside from the obstacles he could not surmount.

Seemingly out of courtesy and consideration for his Congressional followers, the chief executive relaxed his "dictation" during the first few months. But his leaving Congress to frame specifically his general proposals resulted in great disagreement between the two houses, and even among members of his own party. This appeared clearly in the fight over regulating the stock exchanges. Upon returning from his vacation in April, the president served notice that he would apply some of the lessons learned "from the barracuda and the shark." He threatened to tighten the slack and attempted to hasten the adjournment of Congress. He did pull Congress out of deep water, not by being a "tough guy" as he threatened, but by bringing the legislators to plot a course of action under his guidance. The first move after his return was to hold conferences with the House leaders and with important senators. Orders could be issued to the lower chamber, but the president saw the wisdom of co-operating with the chairmen of important Senate committees and with certain senatorial personalities who might endanger his program. Tentative plans were discussed for the remainder of the session. Through conferences of this sort, President Roosevelt during this Congress demonstrated the significance of the presidential office as the only agency for co-ordinating the work of the administrative branches and the legislature. In practice, he evolved informally a "master-ministry" of Congressional leaders, cabinet officers, and executive officials working through the White House.

It seemed that this rather inchoate group of leaders might have developed into a means for increasing co-ordination. The paradox of the present system is that only a conciliatory presidential policy can get the conflicting Congressional blocs to work together—but then to what end? The president likened his tactics to the play-by-play strategy of the football gridiron, but many congressmen preferred to regard him still as another Moses leading the people to the promised land. The matters upon which the President was obliged to compromise or accept defeat were those where a clear group or regional interest was infringed. The measures that he regarded as basic to the recovery program he fought for, but to obtain his ultimate ends he was willing to offer a *quid pro quo.*

This session showed clearly that the representative principle could not be consistently maintained if confusion was to be avoided. A responsible will could be asserted only through skillful use of parliamentary devices for excluding bloc wills. But such procedural tricks were of very limited effectiveness.

The president showed himself an astute politican rather than a crusader. A great burden was placed upon party officials in Congress. No leaders there were capable of securing command by the sheer weight of their personalities. Control was attempted, with only partial success, through the tricks of parliamentary procedure. Congress exemplified the many special interests of class and section, and representative government in these terms cost billions. Although the early New Deal Congresses exhibited, in the main, a picture of president and Congress working together, they also demonstrated how weak are the devices of responsible leadership and control when strained by the divisive force of organized minorities. The presidential system was a game of touch and go between the chief executive and Congressional blocs played by procedural dodges and with bread and circuses for forfeits.

In attempting to evaluate our presidential system in terms of recent experience we must reckon with the fact that an extremely adroit, buoyant, and persuasive politician has been in the White House. Yet the highly tenuous nature of presidential control becomes only too apparent if we recall in careful detail what has happened on those few occasions when an influential group was defied, or a curb on expenditures attempted. The first session of Roosevelt's first Congress provides one example.

The most serious opposition to the president's program arose over the curtailment of veterans' expenditures. Under the authority of the Economy Act (signed March 20), the president issued executive orders for reductions estimated to cut $460,000,000 off the veterans' budget. Accounts of the hardships resulting from these cuts aroused intense dissatisfaction. What the senators objected to, in the words of Senator Long, was "authorizing some little 2-by-4, two-bit job-hunting politician" in the Veterans' Administration to decide the compensation due the ex-service men. "They [the executive orders] went beyond all reason in their reductions," said Senator Dill.

How much opposition to the president by Congress would the public tolerate? It became a matter of percentages in the fight over this measure. One senator proposed to limit cuts in the compensation for service-connected disabilities to 15 per cent. Another thought a 25 per cent limit on reductions might be "put over," while a 15 per cent restriction on cuts would prove too unpopular. "If we insist on cutting off only a small amount," a Senator stated, "and the president should veto the bill, the country will rally to the support of the president and will condemn Congress for undertaking to antagonize his policy." After several proposals had been voted upon, a compromise measure was passed that protected by a 25 per cent reduction limit the compensation of World War veterans with service-connected disabilities and pensioners of other wars. Vice-president Garner voted "yea" to break the tie vote of 42 to 42 and perhaps forestall more drastic amendments. The president objected to this compromise, but the veterans' bloc was ready to demand more. A consultation with House leaders was held, and the president made concessions, relinquishing $100,000,000 from the reductions first contemplated. The House accepted this move but the Senate sought more liberal provisions. Party leaders, fearful of favorable action by the House, immediately called a Democratic caucus and obtained a vote of 170 to 35 in support of the president's position. Conferees were informed that an unsatisfactory conference report would be met with a prompt veto, with all the president's constituents "listening in." The House rejected the Senate proposal, and the Senate finally gave way. References were made to the "party lash" and to telephone calls from the White House urging senators to fall into line. The most persuasive factor, however, seemed to be the feeling that the public had full confidence in the president's sense of justice, and that championing the veterans' cause at the cost of defying the administration would do the ex-service man more harm than good.

This example is cited as illustrative of the necessity of

compromise by the chief executive even at the height of his power. The Congressional calculus must always be in terms of "what will be most effective back home." What percentage of support or opposition is most expedient? This is the mathematics of representative government, and inescapably so, since the ultimate sanction lies in the sum that is struck when the ballots are counted.

The bridge of the separation of powers is popular support for the administration's program. So long as this support is strong and evident Congress will remain docile. What means then has the president for reaching back into the constituency?

A mighty but dangerous weapon in the president's arsenal is his power of going direct to the public over the heads of Congress. The blunderbus may, however, go off in the president's own hands. Nor can such pleas for public support be used often. "A President," Coolidge once said, "cannot, with success, constantly appeal to the country. After a while he will get no response."[9]

Presidents have on occasion encountered public attitudes impregnable to persuasion. No appeal can succeed that runs counter to such firmly grounded beliefs. Constitutionalism and the independence of the judiciary cannot successfully be impugned. The defeat of Roosevelt's court plan is an illustration in point. On another occasion the president wrote to the chairman of the committee considering the Guffey-Snyder coal bill: "I hope your committee will not permit doubt as to the constitutionality, however reasonable, to block the suggested legislation." The chief executive found

[9] Binkley, op. cit., p. 245.

that this was not the way to secure speedy action. His message encouraged opposition and delay. It aroused the constitutionalists. It served to emphasize the difficulty of maintaining smooth working relations between the legislative and executive branches. The president's words served to obstruct his own purpose.

No one can read the record of recent Congresses without clearly seeing that the president's power over the legislative process lay in the force of public confidence behind him. But the president would have been at a great disadvantage if he had relied upon this alone. His tact in handling Congressional leaders was an important factor. His firm threat of veto has proved effective. His bargaining power and his adroit political sense help to explain his Congressional influence.

For weathering the many political vicissitudes of putting through a complicated legislative program the president has a second line of defense. This is his control of patronage. Thus President Roosevelt postponed all appointments except those that could not possibly be delayed, and as a result of this tactic "his relations with Congress were to the very end of the session tinged with a shade of expectancy which is the best part of young love." A president's control of patronage is his most direct means of controlling individual members of Congress. The president can defy pressure groups and appeal to the country over the radio, but when he wishes to marshal Congress behind his program and persuade congressmen to risk the displeasure of important interests in their districts, he needs some means of strengthening their positions at home. The dangers, the faults, and the limitations of this method are obvious. Yet the consummation of a national program of legislation is greatly aided by transmuting through patronage the localism of our politics into support of the chief executive.

The effectiveness of patronage as a means of control is limited by the number of jobs and by the gratitude of job holders. Patronage is not the only weapon of the president; publicity is a third means for control. Both in the White House and in the executive departments, the Roosevelt administration has gone further than any other in systematizing public relations. The president has an invaluable sense of timing. He has demonstrated his acumen for knowing when to appeal to the country. The radio may have a fundamental effect upon the relationship between the president and Congress. By appealing to the people over the head of the legislators, the president may reduce Congress to a body of mere delegates. Without any change in our institutional set-up, publicity through the press and the use of the radio may affect the balance of power in basic fashion.

The relations of the president to Congress can not be dismissed without considering another factor of prime importance. The president's success is not to be explained in terms of patronage or publicity alone. President Roosevelt has been commended for playing Congress with all the skill of an expert fisherman with a trout on his hook. He is certainly more of a fisherman than the late Mr. Coolidge, who fished in kid gloves and approached Congress in the same tentative fashion. President Roosevelt's tactics were adroit, but his fly was more than usually attractive (and expensive).

There is possibility of grave abuse in presidential means for influencing legislation. In patronage lies possible disruption of our administrative service and the death of the merit system. Favoritism, localism, and venality may result from partisan appointments. In official publicity lies the germ of demagoguery in appealing to the mass man who is unable to judge the merits of a controversy. An abuse of the radio appeal is a threat to representative government. Discussion and intelligent criticism are discouraged. Only one side of the case may be understood and that may be misrepresented through overemphasis, understatement, or deliberate omission of evidence. Through the skillful use of patronage and publicity and through the weight of genuine prestige, President Roosevelt was able to control his party support. But not without frequent difficulty. The whole relationship was conditioned by the spending and relief program. Presidential influence in greatest measure must rest upon public confidence, fortified by the chief executive's personal and official prestige with members of Congress.

It was at the level of the presidential office that the hierarchy of party, the confusion of legislative blocs, and the administrative bureaucracy were in some measure co-ordinated for the task of meeting national problems. For leadership in policy, Congress turned to the chief executive. It is an outcome to which one is driven after an examination of past experience. It seems implicit in the nature of our institutional structure.

If chief reliance is to be placed upon the president, the question arises as to the adequacy of his power for carrying such grave responsibilities. The president must be opportunistic, for he is forced to rely upon what is politically expedient. Presidential power depends upon the incumbent's personal influence and upon his manipulative ability plus his capacity to judge the currents of his time and direct these forces into constructive lines. Presidential leadership seems to rest upon a personal rather than a partisan basis. The lack of unity within our political parties means that integrated purpose must be introduced into our political life by a national leader.

To talk of dictatorship is ridiculous in view of the struggles that our presidents have had with Congress in bringing about the relative degree of leadership that has been secured. If there be danger of dictatorship it must be sought in the confusion of the present arrangement and the temptation it offers to the man of action boldly bent upon getting things done. As Coolidge once wrote:

It is because in their hours of timidity the Congress becomes subservient to the importunities of organized minorities that the President comes more and more to stand as the champion of the rights of the whole country.[10]

[10]Calvin Coolidge, "The President Lives under a Multitude of Eyes," 108 *The American Magazine* (August 1929) 146.

Chapter IV

Proposals for Change

So MANY suggestions for changing the relation between the president and Congress have been made from time to time that a brief survey of such proposals is pertinent. Some writers urge that the president be given the power to dissolve the House of Representatives and call a new election in order that the voters may have a choice between Congressional and presidential policy.[1]

If the president were able to threaten to dissolve the House of Representatives, would he find it easier to carry through his program? Incidentally, the Senate is the more recalcitrant branch of Congress today. We cannot discuss in full all the implications such a change in the American Constitution would create. But one important aspect should be noted here. The president would be able to provide a strong point of resistance to group demands. Compromise would thus take place at the presidential level. Special interests that now struggle one with the other in Congress would find it necessary to appeal to the White House when their demands were affected by the presidential program. The ad-

[1]Very interesting proposals for change are found in W. Y. Elliott, *The Need for Constitutional Reform.* (New York: McGraw-Hill Book Company, 1936).

justment of such interests would be dramatized. If an impasse were reached the president could appeal to the nation for support.

If the president were given the power to dissolve the House, a modified form of parliamentary government would be the result. In advocating a change in government it is essential not only to consider constitutional provisions but to examine underlying political forces as well. The effectiveness of a presidential appeal against the protest of Congress would depend upon the response of the nation. If the president possessed a national party machine capable of organizing support for him in all Congressional districts, there would be little doubt as to the outcome. But if pressure groups are sufficiently powerful to conquer Congress, can we assume that they would be markedly less effective in a general election? The answer to our problem cannot be found by pointing to British conditions because the parallel does not hold. The prime minister in Great Britain is the director of a national party machine. He can control the destiny of all candidates enrolled under his party. Their political careers are in the hands of the central party organization. It is said that there is no patronage in the British system. In a strict sense this is true, but through their control of the central party organization the party leaders can choose those who stand for Parliament. This is a kind of superpatronage.

In this country the jobs at the disposal of the party organization are less important. Postmasterships and a multitude of similar governmental posts are used to bring politicians into line with the policy of the party in power. In Great Britain members of Parliament are brought into line before the election takes place; and when there is danger of their rebelling, the prime minister can threaten to call another election. This contingency has a markedly persuasive force because of the centralized control over elections.

In this country the party organization is by no means so unified. A politician identifies his career with a state or even a district. He builds his strength within the locality. The local machine is not dependent upon the national party organization for its vitality. Until our presidents develop national party machines able to cope with local party oligarchies, a president defying the politicians assembled in Congress would be tempting defeat. Under Mr. Farley the Democrats developed a remarkably effective national organization. Whether this is to be permanent remains to be seen. Our national party organization has been essentially a loose confederation of local or state machines. If the president could rely upon a national organization, his power of dissolution might become an effective threat to Congress. Is it wise to create such political backing simply in order to increase the power of the chief executive?

Our experience in the reorganization of state government is sufficient to explode the hope that the answer to our problem would come merely through strengthening the executive arm.

The major premise of the whole movement was: strengthen the governor, put your trust in the governor. It is not unfair to say that some have betrayed the trust. Where reorganization and legislative leadership have failed, it has been largely due to the governor's incompetence. . . . Results have shown that tinkering with the machinery is not enough. . . . The ultimate solution lies beyond the scope of mere institutional reforms.[2]

[2]Leslie Lipson, *The American Governor from Figurehead to Leader*. (Chicago: University of Chicago Press, 1939) 268.

This is the conclusion reached in the latest and fullest study of the efforts made in the states toward increasing the governor's powers.

It does not follow that state efforts toward reorganization are to be passed by; on the contrary, the products of these political laboratories are worthy of close scrutiny. But a broad survey proves that we cannot find an answer to our problems at the federal level simply by giving the president more power—and thereby adding to a burden of responsibility already crushing.

Another suggestion offered many times would give the president power to veto certain items in bills without rejecting the whole measure. The present requirement that he veto all or none of a bill has been criticized particularly with respect to appropriation bills, which are often loaded down with "pork barrel" items which the president may wish to reject. Henry Campbell Black has said that the item veto proposal is a step in "departure from the old theory that the guardianship of the public welfare was vested in the legislature. The new theory would confide it to the executive."[3]

In reality the problem comes down to this: In which branch of the government shall we place our greatest trust, and hence fortify with increased powers?

It must be remembered that the emergency conditions of the last decade have fostered developments responsible for increased executive power. If the president possessed the selective veto this would mean an enormous additional increase in his responsibilities. Legislators would be more prone to give in to the demands of particular interests and

[3]Henry Campbell Black, *The Relation of the Executive Power to Legislation.* (Princeton: Princeton University Press, 1919) 115.

include items with the expectation that the president would veto these undesirable elements. Much of the pressure now exerted on Congress would be transferred to the executive.

The executive power of veto would be cheapened, since its more frequent use on a selective basis would not carry anything like the rebuke to Congress that present presidential disapproval entails. Our chief executive must feel certain of the merits of his action before vetoing an act of Congress. Congress must feel very confident of its position before it overrides a veto. The existing arrangement tends to keep such struggles on a relatively high plane. But suppose the president could strike out any detail of which he disapproved: Congress would become a less responsible body both in its substantive lawmaking and in the ease with which it could find shelter from political difficulties behind the White House.

To be sure, riders in appropriation bills are an abuse. Congress might well observe more strictly the rules that ban extraneous matters in appropriation bills. This would eliminate the occasional annoyance that riders have given in the past; such a reform, however, would not affect the more important balance of legislative and executive branches.

If Congress were better organized for handling its heavy responsibilities we might hear less of the need for increased executive control.

The legislative council is one proposal. Several states have set up such interim bodies composed of experienced legislators aided by experts drawn from administrative agencies. These councils study current policies and prepare a program for the legislature to consider at its next session.

In 1931 the Wisconsin legislature set up an executive council of five senators and five assemblymen appointed by the presiding officers of their respective houses and of ten citizens appointed by the governor.

Illinois has had over two years of experience with a legislative council. Set up in October, 1937, the council has ten members appointed by the president of the Senate and ten selected by the speaker of the House with these two appointing officers serving as ex-officio members. The council studies public policies that have been or should be enacted and prepares a program for the legislature. A research staff is provided. Members of the legislature thus have a body of investigators to whom they may turn for information, and the council has the necessary staff assistance for the development of detailed proposals.

Statutory provisions authorize the council to call upon administrative agencies to make studies. This relationship has been quite important: from it has come valuable factual material. The council is required to be generally proportioned to the strength of the two parties in the legislature, although in practice this requirement has not been adhered to precisely. More important is the fact that the council has not split along partisan lines. But a legislative council cannot escape political influences unless it is willing to play safe by avoiding controversial issues. And if it is to provide genuine legislative leadership, it cannot avoid such questions.

In theory legislative councils as representative bodies are supposed to distill the varied opinions of the parent body and on this basis point the way in policy formulation. This view overlooks the conflict of wills and political forces. As an expert and representative agency, the council is not to seek the unity of will and direction that comes through partisan control.

The Illinois council has not recommended any bills involving important changes in state policy, but it is most significant as a deliberative body. Because of its representative character and the higher degree of education, experience, and ability that can be concentrated in this small group, it can consider more calmly and carefully those measures of state concern that are important but not sufficiently controversial to cause disruption within the council itself. It can maintain close relations with the interests affected by contemplated action and it can consult closely with state officials. The condition under which the council operates encourages more thoughtful consideration than is possible in the heat, hurry, and hub-bub of the regular session. The council's research staff opens channels of information not only for its members but for the legislature as a whole.

The chief conclusion that can be drawn from the experience of our state governments with legislative councils is that they have no place or influence except as they co-operate effectively with the executive branch.

The legislative councils in Kentucky and Connecticut include the governor as an ex-officio member. In Illinois Governor Horner actively co-operated in the establishment of the council, aiding in the selection of the staff and providing aid from his contingency funds in its early period.

The New York Times has urged the creation of a legislative council for Congress.

The advantages of such a device, if adopted by Congress, would be obvious. It would save waste of what for the country might often be precious time. It would permit the President to keep in continuous touch with Congressional sentiment. It would permit him to keep Congressional leaders continuously informed of developments or situations that he regards as important or pressing. It would permit Congressional leaders, on their side, continuously to check and comment upon the actions of the Executive.

Again, it would at once make possible greater co-operation between the President and Congress and greater independence, if Congress desired it, because its own leadership would be more continuous and effective. It would give Congress more time to study proposed legislation. It would allow the country to know in advance what sort of legislation was going to be proposed, so that public opinion would have time to mobilize and crystallize for or against that legislation.[4]

These are weighty reasons deserving serious consideration: heavier tasks for popular government may require not greater power but better designed machinery. The co-operation between a national legislative council and the executive branch might iron out many misunderstandings.

When questions of economy and appropriations come to the fore the existing situation is certainly open to criticism.

The attitude of congressmen toward the voting of federal funds was portrayed by Senator Barkley thus:

I realize how difficult it is to argue against an appropriation out of the Treasury which is designed to help someone. I recall, when I was in the House of Representatives, out in the cloak room one day a very distinguished member of Congress after a heavy lunch was lying on the couch. Someone ran into the cloak room and said, "For God's sake, come out and vote against the amendment. They are about to rob the Treasury of $10,000,000." He jumped up, rushed to the floor of the House, and voted against the $10,000,000 steal as it was portrayed to him. After he

[4]"Continuity in Congress," editorial, *The New York Times,* July 23, 1939 § E, p. 8, cols. 1–2.

had been in the House of Representatives for five or six years, he happened again to be reclining in the cloak room after a heavy lunch, and someone came rushing in and said, "For God's sake come out and vote against an amendment which will rob the federal Treasury of $100,000,000." He merely opened his eyes and turned over and went back to sleep.[5]

The present Director of the Bureau of the Budget, Harold D. Smith, says, "The wall of formality which the separation-of-powers theory has erected between the Executive and Congress needs adjustment where it separates the budgeting and appropriating processes. This process must in its very nature be a joint enterprise of the Executive and Congress."[6]

At present the Congressional committees do not have the immediate benefit of the information gathered by budget officials, nor do representatives of the Bureau participate in a staff capacity during Congressional hearings. The hearings held by the Bureau officials are not attended by men from the Congressional committee staff. No adequate means exists today for acquainting Congress with the mass of information which the executive possesses, and which is so essential in passing judgment on financial needs. Congressmen want more information—formal hearings are insufficient; closer ties between the staff members of the Budget Bureau and Congressional committees seem desirable.

Proposals for a revision of budgetary procedure in the federal government indicate that various members of Congress are aware of the need for improved machinery for the legislative treatment of fiscal policy.

[5]*Congressional Record*, 74th Congress, 1st Session, p. 1849.

[6]Harold D. Smith, Address before the American Political Science Association, Washington, D.C., December 28, 1939.

A budget-review agency has been proposed that would bring together the House Ways and Means Committee, the House Appropriations Committee, the Senate Finance Committee, and the Senate Appropriations Committee. Through this device a broad view of fiscal policy might be attempted. Secretary Morgenthau has endorsed this proposal as follows:

In carrying out our fiscal policy it would be helpful to have machinery which would more fully co-ordinate our efforts. It is not the prerogative of any administrative department to make suggestions to the legislative branch of the Government for the conduct of its work, but I am sure that you would wish me to be frank in suggesting ways of surmounting difficulties which I believe now attend the joint efforts of the Ways and Means and Finance Committees and the Treasury Department.

If, for instance, the Ways and Means and Appropriations Committees of this House and the Finance and Appropriations Committees of the Senate could meet each session as one joint committee on fiscal policy, to consider the over-all aspects of the expenditure and revenue programs, simplification and greater effectiveness would result. The Budget Act of 1921 set up a procedure for the orderly formulation by the Executive of fiscal proposals and for their submission to the Congress as a unified Budget. No comparable procedure has been set up in Congress for considering revenues and expenditures together as two interrelated aspects of a single problem. I hope this committee will agree with me that some such innovation would improve the efficiency of the Government. By providing for a preliminary legislative consideration of the over-all picture of appropriation and revenue measures it would give Congress a broad perspective of the state of the Government's finances and permit a better ordered co-ordination between the executive and the legislative branches in this field. This joint committee would in effect be a lens through which all appropriation and revenue measures could be viewed in relationship both to what the Nation needs and to what the Nation can afford.

This committee should have continuous life for the purpose of actively studying fiscal problems between as well as during sessions of Congress. The Treasury Department would, of course, co-operate in this work to the full extent that the committee desired.[7]

If this plan should be regarded as too far-reaching, senators have proposed that at least the House committees be provided with a staff to study and investigate the proposals in the executive budget.

On January 10, 1940, the Senate passed a Concurrent Resolution to establish a joint Congressional-committee to study budgetary problems. In the debate Senator Adams stated:

It is perfectly proper that the Executive should have a budget committee or bureau to sift out and to study the demands of the departments. But the Congress of the United States needs a budget committee of its own. Congress should have its own investigatory force to undertake an investigation and to check the items.[8]

The debate indicated that the proposal was not without precedent. Several years ago Senator King had tried unsuccessfully to have set up a Congressional budget committee to parallel the work of the executive Budget Bureau. Senator

[7]Revenue Revision—1939. Hearings before the Committee on Ways and Means, House of Representatives, 76th Congress, 1st Session, 1939, p. 3. (Testimony of Morgenthau.)

[8]Congressional Record, January 10, 1940, p. 308. (Statement of Senator Adams.)

Shipstead recalled that he had introduced a joint resolution at a recent session "calling for the establishment of an economic research council to assist the committees of Congress." The Senator said: "When appropriation bills under the budget come to the Committee on Appropriations of either House, we have to take the word of the heads of the departments, and Congress is helpless to check them."[9]

What can be done? The Joint Committee on Internal Revenue Taxation offers one answer. This committee, composed of five members from the Senate Committee on Finance and five from the House Committee on Ways and Means, is assisted by a technical staff. Thus the expertness of lawyers, accountants, and statisticians is made directly available to a committee of Congress. The staff has ten technically trained persons and two stenographers. These experts work with the subcommittees of the two fiscal committees; they consult likewise with Treasury officials and the legislative counsels of Congress. They aid in the drafting of revenue acts. They scrutinize existing tax legislation for loopholes and they watch the administration of revenue statutes. They can be called upon for data to support the views of members of the Joint Committee or to make independent policy recommendations. Taxpayers also come with grievances and suggestions to the committee's staff.

The staff of the committee also seems to feel that it is desirable for it to represent a point of view different from that expressed by the Administrative experts.

While the staff of the Joint Committee undoubtedly fulfills a useful function, a wide extension of similar staff services to other committees of Congress would involve inescapable duplication. It would probably mean frequent differ-

[9] *Ibid.*, p. 309. (Statement of Senator Shipstead.)

ences between the experts hired by Congress and those in administrative offices. Yet it is obvious that congressmen need expert assistance in dealing with the complexities of modern legislation. This need is met in various ways.

Senator Byrd turned to the Brookings Institution for staff assistance in connection with the problem of administrative reorganization. The La Follette Civil Liberties Committee had a staff of investigators recruited for the special purpose of this committee. It has been suggested that one way to foster a closer connection between administrative and legislative branches might be to continue the Temporary National Economic Committee on a permanent basis. Thurman Arnold has stressed the validity of this proposal for the proper enforcement of antitrust problems.

Business should be provided with at least an opportunity to present its contentions before a regularly organized committee with experience in monopoly problems whenever it feels that the existing law prevents efficient operation. And what is true of business men is true of consumers also. Such a tribunal with power to investigate facts and make recommendations to Congress in specific cases could exist anywhere in the government. Nevertheless, it seems to me obvious that the present Temporary National Economic Committee has already established an organization which would be admirable for that purpose. It is the only committee on which there are representatives not only of the Senate and the House but also of executive branches of the government.[10]

Even emergency cannot remove the necessity of Congressional responsibility for expenditures. In fact, critical evalua-

[10]Statement of Thurman W. Arnold, Assistant Attorney General of the United States, before the Temporary National Economic Committee, p. 13.

tion is all the more necessary. For example, we cannot afford to let the admirals have the sole voice in deciding how much money should be spent for airplanes and how much for warships. Issues of war preparation are too important to be left to professional soldiers; the whole economy is involved.

In the field of foreign affairs, as in finance, the relationship between Congress and the executive poses challenging problems. Because of its power to ratify treaties and pass on appointments the Senate is the branch of Congress that is of primary significance. The Senate was originally thought of as a council to which the president might take his problems. But in 1789, when Washington came in person to the Senate to seek advice relative to a treaty with the Southern Indians, it was soon made abundantly clear to him that the senators did not feel his presence conducive to free discussion. There were grumblings, an effort to refer the whole matter to a committee, suggestions for postponement, and finally a tedious debate before the treaty propositions were put to vote. In the process President Washington became so angry that he declared "he would be damned if he ever went there again."[11]

The conception of the Senate as a body with which the president might personally confer has since disappeared, though he confers continually with individual senators on a whole variety of matters. "Senatorial courtesy" stipulates that the president follow the practice of consulting senators of his party about the appointments to be made in their respective states. If the president fails to do so in any instance, as a matter of "courtesy" the other senators will unite in opposing the presidential appointments.

[11]D. F. Fleming, *The Treaty Veto of the American Senate.* (New York: G. P. Putnam's Sons, 1930) 19.

With regard to the ratification of treaties a very strong case can be made against the obstructive tactics of the Senate. The record of history condemns its blindness, but accepting the two-thirds rule for treaty ratification as part of our problem, what can be done to secure better working relations between this body and the chief executive?

Ways of side-stepping senatorial interference have been found. Executive agreements or the use of Joint Resolutions are devices for avoiding the difficulties of treaty ratification. On occasion, the appointment of senators to the commission negotiating treaties is resorted to in the effort to disarm opposition later.

Today it would certainly be futile to argue that the Senate be deprived of its treaty-ratifying power. As Buell points out, "ordinary legislation is now becoming as important as treaties in our dealing with the outside world."[12] The problem is not that of eliminating Senatorial influence but rather of gaining Congressional understanding and support in the whole sphere of foreign relations.

Even if the division of responsibility between the Senate and the president seems at times to frustrate policies thought desirable, there is little present likelihood of changing constitutional provisions. If the president fails to carry Congress along with him, he endangers his policy and fails in his function. It is not enough to have a good policy: equally necessary is Congressional support. President Wilson's behavior in 1918 is the spectacular example of what not to do. He appealed to the country to return a Democratic majority in the impending Congressional elections so that he could go to the Peace Conference with this great supporting mandate behind him. The country did not respond to his plea, but he

[12] R. L. Buell, *Isolated America*. (New York: Alfred A. Knopf, 1940) 451.

nevertheless went ahead as though he had received a vote of confidence. At times he liked to think of himself as a prime minister, but he was not consistent in this role.

The very nature of our system calls for an improved means of maintaining collaboration between the chief executive and Congress. Several proposals were offered at the special session of Congress called in the fall of 1939 to consider neutrality legislation. Senator Davis introduced a bill to set up a National Neutrality Commission. This body would be composed of two members of each party elected by caucus from each house, plus the secretaries of state, treasury, war, navy, and commerce. Senator Davis described the Commission as follows:

The Neutrality Commission would be available at all times, including such times as Congress is not in session. It would be representative of the people as a whole and would be a voice for varying points of view which otherwise would not be heard. . . . It would make for understanding of foreign affairs and yet would not in any way impede or impair the effectiveness of our national defense. It would assure to the people not only the best thought of the executive branch of the government but the considered judgment of the legislative government and would serve as a protection against charges which now fill the air that the Executive is following a policy which will lead the country into war.[13]

Charles Beard has also urged the creation of joint Congressional committees on foreign affairs to maintain close contacts with the president and the state department.[14] Owing to the technical and complicated character of foreign affairs

[13]Bryant Putney, "Participation by Congress in Control of Foreign Policy," *Editorial Research Reports*, November 9, 1939, p. 354.

[14]*Ibid.*, p. 355.

today, Beard contends that a staff of experts attached to this committee could perform a useful function in checking on the experts of the State Department; and where differences of opinion occurred Congress would thus know of the alternative policies open for choice.

No man differs more widely on foreign policy from Charles Beard than does Raymond Leslie Buell, yet on the point under discussion they are in striking agreement. "The immediate need," Buell argues, "is that Congress establish a joint committee of both Houses, possibly containing also representatives of the executive branch of the government and of the general public, to hold hearings and make a study of the international interests of the United States and how the government can best promote them."[15]

Senator Thomas a few years ago urged that the Senate Foreign Relations Committee and the president should work together in the formulation of international policy. This committee of twenty-three members includes the chairmen of other very important Senate committees, and fourteen of its members belong to the party in power. "Surely the day must pass," the senator argued, "when it is easier for the Executive to get agreement with a foreign power than with a committee of his own Senate."[16] Senator Thomas glossed over the fact, however, that the president may represent a very different complex of political factors from that represented by the members of the Senate Committee, who attain their position because of seniority rather than through broad popular election. Only too recent is the neutrality stalemate which occurred when Roosevelt and Hull faced Borah and his confreres. The whole affair was dramatized one evening

[15]Buell, *op. cit.*, p. 452.
[16]*Congressional Record*, Senate, February 1, 1934, p. 1738.

when the key senators from both parties met with the president and his secretary of state in the White House study. Roosevelt outlined the extensive war preparations going on abroad, told of the pessimistic report he had received that very morning from the ambassador to Belgium, and pleaded for a free hand in foreign affairs.

Cordell Hull picked up the narrative when his chief was through, but was presently interrupted by leonine Senator Borah. He, too, he said, receives advices from abroad. Moreover he reads foreign newspapers. He begged to differ with the chiefs of state that war was as imminent abroad as they let themselves think.

Secretary Hull demurred: surely the Senator did not propose to match his sources of intelligence with those of the U.S. State Department? The lion of Idaho, who has never been abroad, denied this implication—but now came a fresh interruption.

The Garner cigar had stopped revolving. The Garner grin was on. His precise words may appear some day in his memoirs. Commonest version reported last week was that, eying the President, the vice-President said:

"All right, Cap'n, we might as well be candid. What's the use of talking about it? You haven't got the votes, have you?"[17]

Without the votes presidential leadership is feckless. Yet, as events subsequently proved, Garner spoke too soon. The president obtained his objective in modified form at the special session of Congress a few weeks later. Senator Borah, with his private line of information, can now cause only a wry smile from the historian. There seems little likelihood of dislodging the Senate Foreign Relations Committee from its entrenched position. It is such vested interests, rather than the separation of powers itself, that lead to stalemate. Instead

[17]34 *Time* (July 31, 1939) 7.

of revamping the document itself we need to appraise certain customs that have grown up under the Constitution. As already noted, seniority is an encrustation that fortifies localism and insulates our representative assemblies from fresh currents of opinion. Can we permit this "cake of custom" to short-circuit the dynamic current of policy? The proposals for change cited in this chapter are worthy of careful thought. It is not fantastic to imagine that out of the experimentation already under way important institutional changes may emerge. The president's custom of consulting with legislators might in time create an informal ministry composed of party leaders in Congress and in the administration.

The very existence of these proposals and experiments is at the least indicative of widespread opinion that further implementation is desirable if our system is to function. The Founding Fathers had few illusions: they had suffered under irresponsible government, they sensed the limitations of unbridled majority rule. They knew that compromise was unavoidable if men were freely to seek their political salvation. The Constitution was contrived by the hands of men who had their fingers crossed. Fascists may salute with upraised palm and communists with clenched fist. Such gestures are denied to citizens who must join hands for self-government.

Chapter V

The President's Entourage

THE president provides the apex for our national political structure—but the organization is not symmetrical, nor is it broadly and evenly based. He must build his own foundations with the means that come to hand. One institution that presidents have used with varying skill is their cabinet. This body is usually thought of as a group of departmental heads who are also advisers on policy. It is questionable whether its chief significance is to be found here. The cabinet offers an opportunity for consolidating political strength through a coalition of leaders whose adherence brings the strength of their political following to the administration.

One proposal that has been made time and again is to permit members of the president's cabinet access to the floor of Congress and the right to speak and answer questions.

The arguments in favor of this plan are as follows: Cabinet members would be the president's chief spokesmen. They could introduce and defend his measures, and by participating in debate they could promote the enactment of a unified program. More versatile and more able men would be attracted to serve in the cabinet. At the same time a closer surveillance of departmental activities would be necessary, since the secretary would be called upon to defend his activities in open debate. In fact, the whole tone of debate would be raised and attention drawn to broad questions of public policy instead of frittered away on political minutiae.

In proposing such a scheme a committee of Congress has stated:

This system will require the selection of the strongest men to be heads of departments, and will require them to be well equipped with the knowledge of their offices. It will also require the strongest men to be the leaders of Congress and participate in debate. It will bring these strong men in contact, perhaps into conflict, to advance the public weal, and thus stimulate their abilities and their efforts, and will thus assuredly result to the good of the country.[1]

The committee sponsoring the proposal that cabinet secretaries be given a seat on the floor of the Senate and House saw in its plan a step toward "sound civil-service reform." They argued that an undersecretary would have to administer the routine of the department since the secretary would be required by his new activities to devote his energies to broad questions of policy.

In 1881 a Senate committee reported favorably a bill to allow cabinet members to occupy seats on the floor of the Senate and the House of Representatives "with the right to participate in debate on matters relating to the business of their respective departments, under such rules as may be prescribed by the Senate and House respectively."[2]

---

[1] Report No. 837 to accompany bill S. 227, 46th Congress, 3d Session, February 4, 1881, p. 8.

[2] *Ibid.*

This proposal came to the fore again when former President Taft supported the idea. He advocated connecting the legislative and executive branches by permitting members of the cabinet to participate in Congressional proceedings. A measure to legalize such procedure was actually debated in the 74th Congress. It was argued that if the course of legislation in the future was to be devised and directed in large measure by the president, existing procedure should be altered to meet this situation.

Despite the irrelevant interruptions of those who tried to interject partisan comments, Representative Harlan ably defended his bill, H. R. 5493.[3] The congressman called attention to the inherent weaknesses in Congressional leadership: able leaders there have been, but "they either voted and talked as the majority in their districts required or they were not re-elected to Congress." "If such leadership happened to be in the national interest," said Congressman Harlan, "it was due to the fortuitous circumstances that a man of exceptional ability happened to come from a district that had the national viewpoint rather than a sectional one. The purpose of bringing cabinet members on the floor of the House is to give the only public official that is elected by all the people of the United States, the President, power to exert leadership over Congress at all times from a national viewpoint; not by the accident of circumstance, but as a system of government." Congressmen remained untouched by what they regarded as an academic discussion.

[3]*Congressional Record,* 74th Congress, 1st Session. See pp. 2758–61, 1999–2002. The first measure of this kind was introduced by Senator G. H. Pendleton in the 46th Congress. Similar attempts to secure such co-operation between cabinet and Congress have been endorsed by three presidents, by a senatorial committee of outstanding ability, and by two chief justices of the Supreme Court (p. 2761). For another interesting view see also Harold Laski, *The American Presidency* (New York, Harper & Brothers, 1940).

Congressman Luce has expressed various objections to allowing cabinet members to participate in the debates of the legislative chambers. He challenges the theory that complete harmony between the branches of government is a good thing in itself. "Something is to be said for the benefits of hostility in moderate degree. Friction has its advantages in state craft as well as in mechanics. The rivalries encouraged by the present system, the antagonisms, yes, even the controversies, invigorate and stimulate."[4]

Much has been said in favor of the question hour in the British Parliament. Without challenging the value it may have under a cabinet system, one may observe that the frequent triviality of the questions is beyond dispute. On the other hand, it offers an opportunity to bring to immediate public attention any phase of administrative policy or activity. However, while many of these questions are used to call the bureaucracy to account, many others are simply used to pester the group in power and to search out weak points for partisan criticism. Transplanting such a system of questioning to the floors of Congress would open up great possibilities for abuses.

We have in our regular Congressional committee hearings and in our special investigating committee procedures ample opportunity for interrogating administrative officials. Moreover, congressmen on behalf of particular constituents go directly to officials with inquiries. Little save partisan purposes would be served in directing such questions to the heads of departments called to account before Congress.

A cabinet member outnumbered by his questioners in Congress would be at a disadvantage; before the public, however,

---

[4]Robert Luce, *Congress, An Explanation.* (Cambridge: Harvard University Press, 1926) 110–11.

he would be likely to find more sympathetic attention. As a statesman "put upon" by Congress his ideas would reach a wide audience. The many-voiced reply of the legislature would be indistinct by its own polyphony. The selection of cabinet members would inevitably be determined by their skill in debate.

It is, moreover, questionable whether the full potentialities of the present cabinet setup have been realized either politically or administratively. Arthur MacMahon feels that "it is hardly an exaggeration . . . to say that for decades hard-driving heads of busy departments have been cynical to the point of resenting Cabinet meetings as a waste of time."[5]
More can probably be accomplished in the direction of smoother co-operation between Congress and the executive by a fuller use of the possibilities existing under the present system than by a formal authorization calling cabinet members into Congress. The opportunities are wide for bolstering the presidential position by the inclusion of factional leaders in the cabinet and by the strategic choice of men with established influence in legislative halls or with the ability to deal efficiently with Congressmen. A brief review of past administrations reveals how effectively and how ineffectively such considerations have been handled by our chief executives.
President Lincoln brought into his cabinet two of his defeated rivals for the presidency. He made his cabinet selections on grounds that were purely political and his cabinet proved to be one of the most successful in our history. Lincoln's campaign managers bargained cabinet posts for

[5]Reprinted from MacMahon and Millet: *Federal Administrators*, p. 5, by permission of Columbia University Press.

convention support: at least three posts were involved, although Lincoln himself denied making any such promises.

Lincoln, accepting the fact that the Republican party was drawn from the Whigs and Democrats, divided his cabinet appointments between these groups. Lincoln's cabinet is a striking example of how a president may strengthen his position through a coalition of factional leaders in the cabinet.

President Grant ignored the growing Liberal Republican element when entering upon his second term; his cabinet reached a new low. Hayes, however, drew heavily upon the reformers in the party but failed to bring in leaders of the other factions.

"Although the Hayes cabinet was an exceptionally able one, it was greatly hampered by the political disagreement between the Executive and Congress."[6] Hayes, in choosing his cabinet, ignored the Congressional triumvirate—Blaine, Conkling, and Cameron. "Grantism" was to go and the make-up of the Hayes cabinet was an indication of the temper of the new administration.[7] The freedom of choice that our presidents have in selecting their advisers is well justified in the case of Hayes. A separation of presidential power from the oligarchy in Congress appeared highly desirable.

Factionalism within the Republican party by the time of Garfield's assumption of office made the selection of the cabinet a task of crucial importance if amicable relations were to be maintained with Congress. Garfield deliberately tried to bring together in his cabinet leaders from the wing of the Republican party to which he owed his nomination and from

[6]Mary Hinsdale, *A History of the President's Cabinet.* (Ann Arbor: George Wahr, 1911) 225.

[7]Claude Fuess, *Carl Schurz.* (New York: Dodd, Mead and Company, 1932) 238.

the Grant wing as well. The result was a coalition comparable to Lincoln's cabinet though its members were lesser personalities.[8]

From the examples cited it is clear that the Cabinet has been a factor in ranging the partisan factions in Congress behind the administration in power. Criticism on this score is hardly in order. Cleveland was politician enough to give more than ordinary recognition to political services in choosing his cabinet. Moreover he selected three senators, a move "favorable to the desired intimacy between Executive and Legislature."[9]

Cleveland and Lincoln could never be accused of lacking in "principles," yet they were aware of the need of building ties with Congress. President Wilson, on the other hand, did not seriously consider making his cabinet a political coalition of factions within his own party; he wanted instead a group of "minds that would travel along with his own." Most of his advisers were strangers to politics as it was played in Washington—political amateurs who may have provided intellectual stamina for his administration, but at the same time made the task of leadership no less difficult. This despite the fact that they worked well together generally.

McAdoo, from his own intimate knowledge of the Cabinet, says:

The weak point of the Wilson Cabinet, it seemed to me, was not in the essential qualities of ability, knowledge, and initiative, but in the matter of political prestige. Most of its members were unknown to the country, and were without political experience or following. From the beginning I saw clearly that the Cabinet

[8]Hinsdale, *op. cit.*, p. 236.
[9]*Ibid.*, p. 247.

would be unable to give the President the effective support which he needed to meet the strenuous opposition that was certain to confront the Administration.

Bryan was the only one of the entire list who had a large and compact following. Burleson was a man of considerable influence among his former colleagues in the House of Representatives, where he had been an important figure, but he was not well known nationally.

William B. Wilson, the Secretary of Labor, was highly regarded by the laboring classes, and was strongly supported by the leading union labor organizations. Franklin K. Lane had some following, but not much, on the Pacific Coast. The rest of the Cabinet, including myself, possessed a very limited political influence.[10]

Harding tried the experiment of having the vice-president attend cabinet meetings, but this did not result in strengthening cabinet ties with the Senate. Nor could this end ever be achieved without drastically changing the characteristic neutrality of the presiding officer of the Senate.[11]

President Coolidge, for all his political acumen, did not take full advantage of the opportunity to get Cabinet members who could be most helpful in Congress. One commentator, writing in 1924, stated:

. . . Mr. Coolidge could find Republican leaders enough in the two Houses to construct a Cabinet that would rank pretty well with the present one in executive ability and above it in effective

---

[10]William G. McAdoo, *Crowded Years.* (Boston: Houghton Mifflin Company, 1931) 192.

[11]From *The Leadership of Congress,* by George Rothwell Brown. Copyright 1922, p. 291. Used by special permission of the publishers, The Bobbs-Merrill Company.

relations with Congress. Mr. Theodore E. Burton, for instance, would probably not have failed with an Administration tax bill in the House, as Mr. Mellon did. Mr. Borah would have known what the result of the Hanihara letter would be on the Senate . . .[12]

Beginning with Lincoln's first cabinet and coming down to 1940, a total of 308 cabinet posts have been filled. (This is counting appointments and not individuals.) In about 25 per cent of these instances the appointee had served in Congress, but much less frequently was a member of the House appointed directly to the cabinet. Over this span of nearly eighty years only twelve Representatives and twenty-one Senators have been brought directly into the cabinet. (See Appendix II.) While the states are widely represented, more than half of the cabinet members come from eight states. It is doubtful that our presidents have made full use of the cabinet as one means of relating the executive and legislature.

Despite the insistence that the cabinet "be put to work," it has failed to function as an institution for the clarification of policy or for the co-ordination of federal activities. In fact, it may be questioned whether the cabinet could perform such duties. It is much more important politically than administratively. If, however, a president appoints men simply because "their minds go along with his," he is not using the cabinet to best effect. The chief executive may surround himself with sympathetic minds by calling upon informal aides. Andrew Jackson had his kitchen cabinet. Coolidge turned to Stearns; Wilson to House.

The president is supposed to stand as the leader of his administration; under him are his loyal cabinet members and

[12]"A Specimen Cabinet," 49 *The World's Work* (December 1924) 123.

the heads of various federal agencies. Actually, members of the cabinet can quietly refuse to co-operate fully. The president might well be unwilling to remove them, since preservation of the appearance of peace within the official family is highly desirable politically. For example, a Jesse Jones can maintain a high degree of independence; politically and administratively, he has remained free and powerful in managing the Reconstruction Finance Corporation. The president has no effective sanction for holding such officials in line. We must look far beyond formal institutional lines if we would understand political relationships.

Usage may be more important than official enactments. From the proposals cited in the preceding chapter it is clear that the separation of powers calls forth many designs for bridging the executive and legislative branches. As we have already noted, many informal means of communication are utilized. One such development has today reached sufficient maturity to be regarded of institutional significance.

Remarkable has been the growth of the staff of officials assisting the president. It is not my purpose to present a full historical account of the evolution of the White House secretariat but rather to call attention to this development as a gradual and unplanned way by which the White House has dealt with the separation of powers.

The office of secretary to the president was established in the McKinley administration. Prior to this, of course, our presidents had their private secretaries, but John Addison Porter, as secretary to President McKinley, regarded his post as worthy of cabinet rank. Porter had taken active part in Connecticut politics and likewise had newspaper interests.

He was a man of wealth and of social position. But he did not know Washington and he was handicapped by ill health. The president came to depend upon his confidential stenographer, George B. Cortelyou, a man of real ability, who soon succeeded Porter. Cortelyou, a career official who was later to hold several cabinet posts, first made his mark in the Post Office, where he came to the attention of President Cleveland. He started at the White House as a stenographer and became in time an executive clerk. Cortelyou, from all accounts, was a man of tact and discernment. He enjoyed McKinley's confidence. In addition to his duties in the executive offices he helped Mrs. McKinley with her correspondence and with the management of social functions.

Under Theodore Roosevelt, Cortelyou became the first Secretary of Commerce and Labor: later he served as Secretary of the Treasury. Here is a striking example of a career administrator whose progress was not arrested by changes in administrations and who served in a confidential capacity under Cleveland, McKinley, and Roosevelt.

Comparable to Cortelyou is the record of William Loeb, Jr. He, too, was a confidential assistant in even more intimate matters. Loeb offered advice and took part in delicate policy and political problems. For example, Theodore Roosevelt stated that Loeb was responsible for starting the investigation into the frauds perpetrated by the Sugar Trust in the New York Custom House. He also had a part in aligning the party convention behind the nomination of Taft. On occasion he shouldered the blame when presidential ventures went awry. For his services Roosevelt appointed him head of the New York Custom House.

According to Arthur Wallace Dunn, a Washington observer, "the successor of William Loeb was as unlike that most successful secretary as a man could be. Carpenter was a self-effacing, patient, painstaking little man."[13] Carpenter had been Taft's secretary in Manila. He was a conscientious man but with no political sense and hence little discrimination in handling callers at the White House. He resigned his office shortly to become the American minister to Morocco.

His successor was Charles Dyer Norton, a former journalist and insurance man who had gained his public experience as assistant secretary in the Treasury. At the time of his appointment, *The Outlook* stated:

The office of secretary to the President is increasingly important, complicated and difficult. It must necessarily be a kind of meeting-ground for the Administration's political relations and the "I want to know" of the public.[14]

Of Mr. Norton it is written that, "with all his acumen and business training, he was as out of place as a raw oyster in a cup of tea. He didn't understand his job and he didn't understand the people with whom he had to deal. He knew even less about politics and politicians than did President Taft."[15] Norton, according to Ike Hoover, "wanted the office of Assistant to the President created, and openly called himself by that title, all with the approval and sanction of the President."[16] Norton also wanted to build up the staff into a permanent group of career officials. His service was brief, however; in less than a year he had accepted the vice-presidency of a large bank. He acted wisely, since his lack of

[13]Arthur Wallace Dunn, *From Harrison to Harding.* (New York: G. P. Putnam's Sons, 1922) II, 101–2.

[14]95 *The Outlook* (June 11, 1910) 275.

[15]55 *Harper's Weekly* (March 18, 1911) 8.

[16]Hoover, *op. cit.,* p. 45.

political acumen had made his position untenable. He proved his ineptitude when, in the summer of 1911, he wrote to one of the Western Republican insurgents confessing that while the president had withheld patronage in order to get them into line, such coercion would not be used in the future. The public furor that greeted the publication of such a letter from the White House can be imagined. It is said that this letter "fairly settled Mr. Norton's business so far as making a success of the secretaryship was concerned."[17]

In appointing a successor to Norton, President Taft selected a man with demonstrated capacity for dealing with Congress. Charles Dewey Hilles had served as the assistant secretary of the Treasury in charge of the construction of public buildings. Often the selection of a site greatly interests local politicians, and Mr. Hilles had made many intimate contacts with members of Congress. He gained a reputation for "circumspection and impartiality" in his Treasury post. Nevertheless, about a year later, Taft was again on the search for a secretary.

Not until August, 1912, with the appointment of Carmi Thompson did Taft bring to the White House a secretary with experience in both elective and administrative office. Carmi Thompson had been assistant secretary of the interior for two years; prior to this he had been secretary of state for Ohio and speaker of the Ohio House of Representatives. He had also served in Congress. At the time of Thompson's appointment, *The Independent* stated:

The position of Secretary to the President is very different from what it used to be, and very different from an ordinary secretaryship. It is no longer a station at the President's elbow,

[17]55 *Harper's Weekly, op. cit.,* p. 8.

with pad and pencil for dictation, and readiness for errand-boy service. It is a position of responsibility and brain work hardly second in demands to that of the President himself. Lamont, Cortelyou, Loeb lifted the position higher and higher till it is a fact, today, that the ability of the secretary and his direct and indirect influence, make a vast difference in the success of the President's administration.[18]

Woodrow Wilson was served by the faithful Joseph P. Tumulty while governor of New Jersey and throughout his two terms in the White House.[19]

President Harding, in characteristic fashion, took to Washington as secretary G. B. Christian, an old friend and neighbor of Marion, Ohio. Although a Democrat, Christian was among the first to support Harding in his political career. He became secretary to Senator Harding in 1915 and accompanied his employer to the White House.[20]

Coolidge's appointment of Bascom Slemp was dictated not by the sentiment and personal attachment that explains similar presidential appointments, but was a shrewd and calculated political move. Slemp was a Virginia politician. He was an influential figure among southern Republicans and his handling of patronage for the Republican National Committee had occasioned some criticism. "But he knew his way around in Washington," William Allen White explains.

His party status had not been questioned. His personal integrity was not at issue, however keenly his political activity had

[18]73 *The Independent* (August 15, 1912) 363.

[19]Consult Joseph P. Tumulty, *Woodrow Wilson as I Knew Him*, and R. S. Baker for evidence on Tumulty relations.

[20]Samuel Hopkins Adams, *Incredible Era*. (Boston: Houghton Mifflin Company, 1939) *passim*.

been criticized by those who had no great love for the Republican party. Slemp was the man whom President Coolidge needed, a liaison officer between the White House and the Republican organization in Congress and in the National Committee, a man "diligent in his business" who should stand before kings. From the Democratic press, from the independent press, from the Progressive group in Congress and out, a storm of protest rose over Slemp, but it beat vainly upon the White House. The new president knew exactly what he wanted and he had it.[21]

Coolidge made another appointment equally well based on sound political considerations. He wanted at his right hand "a man thoroughly conversant with conditions in Congress and with the Congressional mind."[22] Coolidge had known Everett Sanders from his Amherst years. The latter, who had been a member of Congress from Indiana from 1917 to 1925, in 1924 had directed the Speakers' Bureau for the Republican National Committee.

Hoover followed Coolidge's example in designating a secretary especially qualified to deal with Congress. One journalist has pictured this secretary as follows:

The Hon. Mr. Newton is another link in the Hoover system of pipe-lines everywhere. Through his contacts in Congress Mr. Hoover gets confidential information on what is going on behind the scenes on the Hill. He also uses Mr. Newton to examine the activities of the various independent commissions and boards and to keep a check on the departments. But most important of all, Mr. Newton and the altruistic Mr. Burke handle patronage. They are both well chosen for this work. Mr. Newton is the

[21]William Allen White, *A Puritan in Babylon.* (New York: The Macmillan Company, 1938) 251.

[22]*The New York Times,* January 15, 1925, p. 1.

perfect type of Farm Belt politician. He talks much about the need of Farm Relief and yet when he was in the House he voted for the Hawley tariff bill, one of the most bold-faced steals ever attempted on the farmer, and against the debenture plan, a device which would have applied the tariff principle to agricultural exports.[23]

Hoover had two other secretaries besides Newton. This threefold division of labor suggests the three aspects of the presidential office that are of most importance: relations with Congress, with the press, and with the administrative services. George Akerson was the secretary who met the newspapermen. Lawrence Richey has been regarded as a rather mysterious figure charged with confidential missions to stop criticism or to investigate special situations. Richey's direct responsibility was to act as a go-between for the president and the administrative services.

Of particular interest was the announcement that Newton would have "charge of appointments to places other than in the Post Office Department." This secretary, together with Postmaster General Brown and James F. Burke, counselor of the Republican National Committee, was to supervise a reorganization of the party in the South. This was about as close as the papers could come to explaining that the secretary in charge of patronage would take appropriate steps to keep Congress in line.

The increased size of the White House staff that occurred under Franklin D. Roosevelt was but a further development of existing trends.

"For the toughest job on earth" the chief executive needs

[23]A Washington Correspondent, "The Secretariat," 18, No. 72 *The American Mercury* (December 1929) 391.

ample assistance. Woodrow Wilson had a clerical staff of forty. Today more than two hundred are employed in the White House. Heading the organization are the three secretaries to the president. Stephen Early has been described as the Louis Howe of the present administration and Roosevelt's chief "no" man. Brigadier General Edward M. Watson, the president's military aide, serves as buffer between Roosevelt and department officials who insist that they can discuss their problems only with the president. Nor is the "missionary work" which Early and Watson both perform in dealing with members of the Senate and the House their least significant service to the chief executive. The third secretary, William D. Hasset, is literary research man for the president.[24]

Formally the activities of the three secretaries are explicitly outlined: one each to handle the public, the Congress, the press and radio. Actually their work cuts across these lines of division. Each secretary has his assistants and these are quickly shifted from one office to another as the load of work demands.

It is questionable whether the president's personal staff can be further formalized and still maintain its usefulness. The relationships between the chief executive and his immediate entourage are bound to reflect the personality traits of the "Chief." The determining fact is not simply what is good administrative practice, but what kind of setup is preferred by the president. What would be workable under one president might not prove feasible for his successor.

The president's assistants co-operate with cabinet secretaries when the latter seem willing. The president needs direct and neutral channels of information; these things his assistants try to provide.

[24]*The New York Times,* July 23, 1939.

While quiet sabotage by unsympathetic technicians and genteel blackmail by high policy officials can take place silently within an administration, the chief executive is at least in a better position to offset these tendencies if he can keep himself informed about what is going on. Hence the president's administrative assistants can perform a useful function by keeping him in touch with events within his administration. Most administrative activity is routinized, but scattered unevenly throughout the bureaus and services are officials engaged in planning, analysis, and policy formulation. Here is the administration's nervous system. These officials are not directed by the kind of reflex action that controls so much bureaucratic activity. It is important that the president be informed of the thinking that is being done in these more active areas of policy. Theoretically it might be supposed that cabinet officials would report on such matters to the president, but these secretaries likewise have difficulty in keeping informed of all that is happening in their vast departments.

Even more difficult to control than the divergencies that may develop among the policy makers of an administration are the resistances that may be offered by officials combining technical *expertise* and important managerial duties. When a high policy official is told by his subordinates that a projected policy is technically unsound or administratively impractical, his plans may be brought to a standstill.

Of especial importance are the developments resulting from the recommendations of the President's Committee on Administrative Management. At the very beginning of its report, the President's Committee on Administrative Management stated: "The President needs help."

The Committee proposed that the president be given six

administrative assistants in addition to his existing staff. These were definitely not to be regarded as "assistant presidents in any sense." Their function rather would be to gather all pertinent information for the president, and to provide liaison between the executive office and other agencies, including Congress. The Committee likewise urged that the federal agencies be attached to the White House that were concerned with the staff functions of personnel administration, fiscal management, and planning. While the full recommendations of the Committee have not been realized in all their details, their suggestions have been substantially followed. Real advances have been made in the development of the White House staff. The president has able assistants now, and he can add others when he so desires. The Bureau of the Budget is now virtually part of the White House secretariat; the National Resources Board and the Central Statistical Board have been brought in as planning and coordinating agencies. The Division of Government Reports, formerly the United States Information Service, is now attached to the executive office. These changes in the staffing of the White House suggest that the president is developing into a real administrator in chief.

The inertia generated by large-scale organization is tremendous. It is such inherent factors that draw invisible limits around the Chief Executive's effective sphere of control. If the president is to be effective, there must be numerous individuals working throughout the government who share deeply the purposes typified by their chief. Through his White House staff, through his cabinet, and through his supporters in Congress presidential influence must weld policy despite the separation of power.

Chapter VI

The Limits of Presidential Responsibility

THERE is in fact a real limit on the agencies to which the president can give thought. A dynamic chief executive may be able to hold much of the bureaucracy in control, but our administrative system is not constructed as a symmetrical pyramid with all lines headed up at the apex of the chief executive. As Lindsay Rogers states: " . . . Throughout much of the administrative field, the President is unable to initiate or to prevent. The heads of departments and independent establishments have authority which is theirs to use without the necessity of securing presidential approval."[1]

To stand generally accountable for the whole, even though he lacks control over all the parts, a presidential commander in chief is elected for a four-year term. Though battles may be lost, no provision is made for a better tactician until the sands of time have run their allotted course. Since this is the nature of our government it follows that the president, if he is to remain effective and if he is to hold the confidence of the voters, must maintain some of the detachment of a

---

[1] Lindsay Rogers, "The American Presidential System," *Political Quarterly* (October–December 1937) 524–25.

constitutional ruler. On the other hand, he is expected to formulate policy and see to its execution. Through close identification of policies or actions which the voters may decide to repudiate, he runs the constant danger of becoming discredited before his term of office has expired. In halcyon times a discredited occupant of the White House is an inconvenience; in times of emergency such institutionalized futility may become tragic.

As one way in which the dilemma may be partially avoided, the president may act as a generalissimo who devolves upon his generals the responsibility for the attainment of particular objectives. If they fail they can be disgraced and removed; or kicked upstairs to posts of less crucial importance. The generalissimo is expected to win the war; he can lose some battles in the process. The chief executive must be held responsible for the attainment of very broad objectives: to be effective, however, he cannot carry the full burden of accumulated grievances that follow from many minor defeats. Hence, as part of the price of effective presidential leadership, lesser officials must be held accountable for particular policies.

As one example of this kind of relationship an incident is found in President Franklin D. Roosevelt's tax program in the first session of the 74th Congress. His tax proposals came as the culmination to a "must" program that had aroused increasing protest from various quarters. Hostile senators interpreted the president's tax message as "a political gesture intended to offset the great public alarm and the very great interest in the share-the-wealth movement." The message came on Wednesday, June 18, 1935, and by the week end general confusion prevailed as to what should be done: Senator Harrison and Representative Doughton, chairmen

respectively of the Senate and the House Ways and Means
Committees, were reported as opposed to tax legislation at
this session; Speaker Byrns and Floor Leader Robinson
favored action before adjournment. After a three-hour conference at the White House, the newspapers quoted Robinson as saying that "it was decided to press for action on the
recommendations of the President as to amendments to the
tax laws at the present session."

Senate leaders considered expediting the president's program by adding it as an amendment to the nuisance-tax bill
then before the Senate and which would have to be passed
by June 30 if the nuisance-tax provisions were not to lapse.
The public reaction to such a speedy consummation, however, was unfavorable. The president was asked at a press
conference whether the collection of nuisance taxes would
cease in case the resolution authorizing their continuance
was held up by his tax program. He denied that he had
urged or requested the enactment of his tax program by
midnight on Saturday, June 30. His recommendations, he
said, had dealt merely with principle and policy. Critics took
this to mean that the president had shifted his position to
avoid criticism. Robinson and Harrison, who had promised
immediate action, were placed in an embarrassing position.
"What irritates me," said Senator Hastings, "is that the
President of the United States, because of the loyalty of
these two great men, should make them take the blame instead of taking it himself." Had the president left his loyal
ministers sitting out on a limb? Had the chief executive
backed down? Senator Harrison denied that this was the
case. He explained that he favored adding the tax program
as an amendment to the nuisance tax because he felt that
this was the "only way" to have the matter considered at the

present session. Then he found that certain "tax experts" were not ready to advise the Finance Committee and that a delay was inevitable. "I immediately got in touch with the leader of the House," Senator Harrison stated. "I spent hours over at the other end of the Capitol in conference with Speaker Byrns, with Chairman Doughton, and with the whole Democratic membership of the Ways and Means Committee. I told them the whole situation." It was agreed to pass a joint resolution continuing the nuisance taxes for sixty days and then to take up the president's tax program. Thus, "seemingly undue haste" might be avoided.

Was the unfavorable public reaction to hasty legislation too powerful to be ignored? Did the question of constitutional propriety in "initiating" the tax program in the Senate enter into the change of front? Was the delay of the "experts" the real reason? Or had the president changed his mind? "Whatever wrongdoing has been committed," protested Senator Harrison, "whatever erroneous impressions may have gone to the country, we do not blame the President of the United States." To some members of the Senate it appeared that the senator did "protest too much."

The significance of this incident does not lie in the hidden motives of the participants, whatever they may have been, but rather in the fact that our presidential system has produced ministers who are ready to take public blame in order to shield the chief executive. The episode raises a question as to the wisdom of making the presidential office more responsible. If the president were held to a closer accountability, he would inevitably become laden with an accumulation of grievances. Is this compatible with an official elected for a fixed term of years? F. J. Goodnow once described the English prime minister as "so sensitive to public opinion

that the work of a day almost may cause his overthrow."[2]
More than one official in both the legislative and administrative branches have drawn upon themselves the opprobrium that under a parliamentary system would be directed at the prime minister. When a political party hopes to maintain its leader in the White House for eight years, the president must be guarded from the frictions that his administration creates. The New Deal has had a notable procession of scapegoats who have retreated from office under a weight of popular disapproval. The president would cease to be effective if he had to bear this burden alone. If he loses his influence over Congress and his popularity throughout the country, his constitutional powers avail him little. A characteristic of our presidential system seems to be this tendency to shield the chief executive and hence to divest the presidential office of an overwhelming weight of responsibility. To what extent responsible executive control is compatible with our presidential system with its fixed tenure of office is certainly debatable. In this country it is not an easy task to distinguish between those acts for which the president should be held answerable and those over which he has no control. The critic who would hit the guilty party must use buckshot.

If we turn from legislative tactics to the administrative field we find that numerous regulatory bodies set up by Congress and answerable to it result in a considerable devolution of authority. From this point of view the existence of independent commissions, while sometimes inconvenient

[2]Frank J. Goodnow, *Politics and Administration.* (New York: The Macmillan Company, 1900) 261–62.

to presidential policy, may yet relieve the chief executive of a greater burden of political responsibility than any one man can effectively carry. While as a matter of theory it may be desirable to limit the number of independent agencies and hold them to their original purpose, we are not likely to attain such consistency in actual practice. The administrative branch of government has proliferated widely as one answer to the inadequacies of the judicial and legislative branches. "It represents," Landis states, "our effort to find an answer to those inadequacies by some other method than merely increasing executive power. If the doctrine of the separation of power implies division, it also implies balance, and balance calls for equality. The creation of administrative power may be the means for the preservation of that balance, so that paradoxically enough, though it may seem in theoretic violation of the doctrine of the separation of power, it may in matter of fact be the means for the preservation of the content of that doctrine."[3]

Two questionable assumptions are often made by those who criticize our form of government for lack of direction. They assume the purpose of the state to be the expression of the "will of the people" and they assume that if the government were better constructed it could then carry out the "correct policy." One need hardly point out that no necessary connection exists between what the people may be thought to desire and what experts are likely to prescribe. The concept of "experts" and that of "people" are altogether too simple to prove useful for purposes of analysis.

The actual problem for legislators and administrators alike is not to express an assumed single popular will but rather

[3]James M. Landis, *The Administrative Process*. (New Haven: Yale University Press, 1938) 48.

to devise a working adjustment of the conflicting wills of men as they are expressed in their group loyalties. Likewise, the politician cannot turn to the "experts" for a unanimous judgment. Experts of great technical competence often disagree, and usually a politician can secure support for his own side from those technicians who happen also to be fellow partisans. To be sure, there are fields where scientific precision is so far advanced that only one answer is defensible, but this is not the case with regard to the questions that are the occasion of so much policy controversy today. Experts may investigate, analyze, and suggest alternative methods of treatment, but they cannot speak with finality where the government faces industry.

These limitations are habitually overlooked by those who are impatient with the alleged slowness of existing democratic procedures. If Congress were composed exclusively of social scientists, it would still be a political body, and parties and blocs would inevitably arise. The area wherein men struggle for prestige and advancement does not furnish the conditions most suitable to considering the substance of public policy. Political struggle for office is important, but chiefly as a means of keeping officeholders aware that their continued power is contingent on popular support.

Special interests prefer to see special administrative agencies set up to symbolize or execute their special purpose. This is one explanation for the multiplicity of so-called independent executive agencies. A good case can be made for an independent commission charged with judicial powers; but much less defensible are the bodies of a promotional or purely administrative nature. Interests building on their affinity for the agency with which they are most familiar may urge the assumption of duties that have little to do with the original responsibility of the agency. Thus the I.C.C. has been burdened with purely administrative tasks, such as safety regulation, or strictly judicial activities, such as action in bankruptcy matters, neither of which relates to its primary duty of rate regulation. In other words, there is a tendency for our quasi-judicial commissions to grow into ministries. They become enmeshed in fields of public policy far transcending their judicial duties. Is it chimerical to hope that in time a greater degree of balance can be attained? It will certainly be a long time before the consumer interest is brought into balance with producer interests within the administrative branch, but notable advances have been made in strengthening labor's voice. The aged and the handicapped now have their administrative defenders.

Successful policy formulation demands both accurate representation and informed judgment. Thus the farmers' opinions today are brought into the governing process not only through an agricultural bloc in Congress but also through extended and systematic contacts between officials of the Department of Agriculture and hundreds of thousands of farmers in their own communities. In this man-to-man contact, theories of the separation of powers seem empty indeed. The farm-relief movement is that complex of attitudes and interests working together over a long period toward a goal that can be defined broadly but realized concretely only as temporary *modi operandi* are devised. But their general long-range objective holds together men from different farm organizations and officials drawn from state, local, and federal agencies. This movement is so impelling that the separations of public and private jurisdictions or legislative and administrative branches are blurred in the more imperative focus of how to help the farmer.

Our society has many such movements differing in degree of continuity and of intensity, but sufficiently dynamic to charge the separated branches of our governmental machinery with a current that produces common action for a common cause. Thus continuity in public policy is to be found not in party programs but in these broader movements which promote such causes as farm relief, labor unionism, social security, national defense, public health, child welfare, old-age protection, sound money, protectionism, conservatism, etc. Giving life to these objectives are groups of individuals determined to hold the lines of separated political agencies together long enough to accomplish their aims. What, then, is the validity of the separation-of-powers concept?

This theory, according to some writers, originally identified the major branches of government with the chief economic and social forces in the community. Thus, John Adams visualized one house of the legislature as representing the masses; the other, the aristocracy. Under a monarchy the crown clearly had a different social and economic basis from that of the Commons. Both executive and legislature today are broadly representative. They can hardly be treated as counterbalancing social classes. Governmental agencies for channeling class or group interests are found rather within the administrative branch.

Politicians and administrators, to be effective conciliators, must not be too directly identified with any one of the interests among which they must negotiate. Some degree of neutrality as between competing groups is insured for the administrator by his status in a well-established administrative service, and for the politician by association with his political party. To the extent that politicians or administrators are really spokesmen of special interests, thinly disguised under the cloak of their official function, their usefulness as winners of consent is reduced.

The point is this: If social and economic differences are to be reconciled through discussion (which is the essence of the democratic process), then this cannot be left to the debates that take place in legislative assemblies. Here checks and balances can only be tolerated as minor procedure devices for protection against careless and hasty action. In broader social terms a checking and balancing of interests must take place not to the end of forestalling action but for the purpose of developing an integration of point of view on questions of public policy. The administrative branch can play an important part in the process. We can find instances where a fusing of pressure into the common purpose of policy has taken place through the administrative branch. Two recent examples are the Special Committee on Farm Tenancy and the Advisory Council on Social Security.

The Special Committee on Farm Tenancy offers the example of a form of procedure that brings together all the interested groups. President Roosevelt, in November, 1936, asked Secretary Wallace to serve as chairman of a special committee to prepare "a long-term program of action to alleviate the shortcomings of our farm tenancy system." The president instructed the committee to consult with Senator John H. Bankhead and Representative Marvin Jones, as well as to secure the views of other state and national leaders. The Special Committee on Farm Tenancy was composed of leaders of farm organizations, editors of agricultural newspapers, educators, officers of social welfare agencies, and federal officials. This committee, appointed in November and requested to report about two months later, could not have responded had not experts already collected much of the pertinent data. Moreover, a technical committee of agricultural economists set up by the Special Committee and the National Resources Committee actually prepared the text of the report. The Special Committee on Farm Tenancy, however, held hearings at five regional centers where the tenancy problem was very severe. They consulted with a special advisory committee of the National Resources Committee. In the final report of the Committee there was little dissent. The chairman of the House Committee on Agriculture was eager to have copies of the full report made available for his committee and the ultimate educational effect of the report was stressed.

In the process of policy formulation exemplified by the farm tenancy problem means were deliberately sought for securing a meeting of minds among officials and agricultural leaders. The Committee served to convert the data of experts into an action program acceptable to Congress. The rigidities of a separation of power were rendered meaningless. The Committee was confronted by a real problem in the face of which rivalries between legislative and executive branches seemed unimportant. Yet the tactical need for cooperation was not overlooked.

The Advisory Council on Social Security served as another means of bringing together about a common problem the various parties at interest. This Advisory Council included six representatives of employers, six of employees, and thirteen of the public. The Council was appointed by the Social Security Board and the Senate Special Committee on Social Security, in May, 1937. This special committee had been designated by the Chairman of the Senate Committee on Finance. Officials were detailed from the Board to give research assistance to the Council. An Interim Committee of the Council prepared the agenda for the less frequent plenary meetings. Individual members of the Council were provided with documents and reports by both the Social Security Board and the Interim Committee. The whole committee met about six times between November, 1937, and December, 1938.

Officials from the Social Security Board consulted with the Council, and experts from the Treasury and Post Office departments were called in for special problems. Members of the Senate Special Committee offered advice. The Council reported that "it also studied the proposals concerning old-age security advanced by a large number of bodies representing industry, labor, professional, social welfare, and general-citizen groups."[4]

The sessions of the Council served to clarify the ideas of all who participated. In the course of these meetings leaders in business and labor circles gained a new understanding of social security problems and found their ideas enlarged and modified by the very process of discussion. This educational experience was shared by the Board. The Council raised questions for the Board's technicians to work out. This necessitated thorough study in order to prepare a report for the next meeting of the Council. Problems were raised which forced the Board to envisage various possible future alternatives which could only be analyzed by gathering extensive actuarial data. When the report of the Council was finally made after a year of activity, it was well received by Senator Vandenberg and his colleagues, even though they did not

[4]Advisory Council on Social Security, Final Report, December 10, 1938, p. 7.

agree in all instances with its recommendations. The question of old-age reserves was the one big point upon which Congress ultimately overrode the Council's recommendations. In general, Congress followed the Council's proposals, which were in fact closely parallel to those of the Social Security Board itself.

In addition to the educational influence of the Council upon its own participants and upon Congress and the Board, a marked shift in newspaper opinion was discerned. Editorial comments reflected a better understanding of social security problems. This was concrete evidence of a broader influence which the Council's activities undoubtedly had in the mind of many thoughtful citizens.

Our experience with this Advisory Council seems to justify further use of such procedures in dealing with controversial issues. Here were representative leaders and experts called together to advise with administrators and forced to buckle down to concrete questions. They engaged in a process which enabled them to clarify their own views and required them to put their names to specific recommendations for action. The prestige of the group carried weight, and its final recommendations served to modify the views of extremists.

The *ad hoc* nature of the Council is a fact of real significance. A group of citizens or experts serving together as a continuing agency tends to become labeled in the minds of the public with a particular set of attitudes. If the members meet with reverses in their recommendations, their opinions may become discounted. An *ad hoc* agency brings new points of view to the problem. Once its immediate usefulness is served it is disbanded. There is no danger of its attempting to justify its existence, and public confidence is probably increased.

The experience of this Council bears out a comment of John Gaus: "Authority, in short, follows the successful exercise of function; the role of the administrator is to achieve a reconciliation of the interests involved, and requires the winning of consent by the accumulation of exact and relevant knowledge."[5]

A growing recognition of the importance of the administrator in the "winning of consents" prompts the hope that through this channel will come a most important contribution to the solution of our problem. Interests must be well on the road to reconciliation before we can dare to leave them to the bickering of partisans.

Concretely what does this mean? It means, for example, that employers and employees cannot safely wait until their respective champions clash in forensic battle in Congress— the loser to bow meekly to the conqueror. It means that when problems of wage rates, industrial costs, market controls, and the like, promise ultimately to precipitate political conflicts, the parties at interest would be well advised to start negotiations immediately. Perhaps conflict can be headed off quickly; if not, at least a wide factual basis can be constructed and each side educated to the other's point of view before the problem becomes a political issue.

The Swedes have been particularly successful in their use of Royal Commissions. These agencies bring together representatives of all the special interests involved and they, together with experts and government officials, carry on prolonged debate and investigation. All this is done without publicity, and agreement on principles is sought before any reports are made to the press or to Parliament. By the time

[5]John Gaus, *Frontiers of Public Administration.* (Chicago: University of Chicago Press, 1936) 39.

the political stage for open political debate is reached the issues have been reduced to questions of detail and procedure.

Giving the president formal powers for overruling Congress offers no solution any more than would procedural dodges for increasing Congressional authority. Appealing to the general electorate to decide between the two fails to meet the real question. The crux of the matter is adjustment. This calls for *expertise* exercised with patience and subtlety; it calls for the highest intelligence in the discovery of new ways and means. You cannot settle a technical question of engineering by a show of hands; questions of human engineering are no less intricate.

The dramatic stalemates between Congress and president have occurred when grave problems have confronted the two branches of government without the preliminary period of discussion essential to the formation of an integral result. The way to meet the separation-of-powers dilemma of our system is to provide a preliminary process of discussion that will iron out the major points of dispute. The crises that have occurred in the relations between the president and Congress are symptoms of much deeper differences. We must try to reach these levels of adjustment.

Cleveland, treating tariff reduction as a great and simple moral question (instead of an enormous complex of economic interrelationships), defied Congress to do his will. He met defeat. Wilson, treating world reorganization as a crusade for justice to be ratified by a great act of faith, was overwhelmed by a Congress holding different views on how to further justice and promote security. Hoover, facing an economic disruption of vast magnitude, met a defiant Congress. The difficulties in all such cases reach back into the fears and the uncertainties of the community itself. The democratic process proved inadequate to bring the people quickly to a unified response. The president appealed to the country, but his influence was insufficient; apparently a majority of the representatives in Congress felt that a majority of their constituents were unmoved by the presidential policy. And in the light of subsequent events the repudiated presidential policies remain debatable.

It is most desirable to find some way of promoting a meeting of minds of administrators and legislators before political debate becomes overheated.

Close connection between administration and Congress is extremely important in the framing of technical legislation. Administrators, after years of study and experience, may know deeply and sincerely that certain changes in a statute are essential to successful administration. But how are they within the space of an hour or two of testimony able to compress their knowledge and convictions into the form that will be convincing to a Congressional committee? Even if the congressmen on the committee have some familiarity with the general problems of the administrative agency, they can have little understanding of the intricacies of carrying out the policy. And it is often this experience that has educated the administrator to his own understanding of the problem. How can he share this education with the politician who is to make the decision?

Other administrative recommendations may be the result of careful compromise. After prolonged negotiation between officials and interested groups, certain terms have been agreed upon. If Congress casually upsets the agreement thus reached the administrator becomes suspect. Private groups may accuse him of a breach of faith. Congressional hearings are often a quite inadequate medium through which an official may give legislators an understanding of the process by which the compromise was reached. In a two-hour lecture the nuances that led to the particular compromise cannot be put adequately before the Congressional committeemen. If this is the result, the hearings create a hiatus in the democratic process of adjustment. Of course this is not always the case, but the opinion is expressed that some more continuing relationship should be worked out between administrators and legislative committees.

Much of the apparent ineptitude of our government has arisen from the failure of officials to consult with members of Congress. The problem is as simple as this. A little more tact; a little less impatience; a readiness to share the prestige of sponsoring a new idea for legislation: through such minor concessions most of that no-man's land between politicians and bureaucrats could be abolished. This is the opinion voiced by experienced observers in Washington. In fact, our system would not work if there were not habitual co-operation. The failures at agreement constitute the dramatic quarrels and stalemates that result in sharp suspicion concerning the present adequacy of the whole system. Because the squabbles of man and wife sometimes lead to marital disaster does not warrant either the general abolition of marriage or the outlawing of divorce. The Constitution joins the president and Congress for better or for worse. But there is no pledge to love, honor *and* obey.

Chapter VII

The Strength of Presidential Leadership

Wᴇ ᴄᴀɴɴᴏᴛ invest in our chief magistrate the sole responsibility for wise policy and effective administration except in a symbolic sense. The paradox of our system rests in the fact that the presidency is the symbol of national unity; yet, as we have indicated, national organizational support is lacking.

There are no really adequate sanctions for forcing Congressional compliance. Such controls are essential to parliamentary government.

The prime minister, standing at the apex of a disciplined party machine, holds the power of political life or death over his followers. He can call for an election under circumstances most favorable to himself; he can control the electioneering process and campaign funds. The M.P. is hardy indeed who defies the party hierarchy. "To vote down the Ministry is to vote one's self out of a seat and one's party out of power," Howard Lee McBain wrote. "It is to play with uncertainty, to stake the future on a problematical throw of the political dice. Small wonder that the Commons is docile under domination. Cabinet responsibility is a threadbare legal conceit."[1] These are strong words, yet events in the dozen years since they were written add strong evidence. For all his ineptitude in the events leading up to Munich and beyond, Chamberlain maintained his position. That he could hold on so long was Great Britain's tragedy.

Presidential government, despite frequent predictions to the contrary, has functioned without strong partisan controls. A. Lawrence Lowell, in his exhaustive study on "The Influence of Party upon Legislation,"[2] discovered that party voting steadily increased in the House of Commons from the middle of the last century. "The tendency of the parliamentary system in its development was toward more and more strict party voting." The situation in the United States is quite different. Mr. Lowell proved that "the amount of party voting varies very much from one Congress, and even from one session, to another and does not follow closely any fixed law of evolution. . . ." In Great Britain the duty of the opposition is to oppose. It is the whole tendency of the system that distinctive parties govern the nation in accordance with the class basis upon which their strength is organized. If control by class parties is pushed to its logical conclusion, government by discussion becomes impossible. Irreconcilables face each other across an abyss of divergent interests. The isolation of classes into separate parties prevents that modification of extreme points of view that is possible when different elements join in compromise. The results of the British Conservative party in encouraging German armament because of a fear of Communism are now apparent. Parliamentary government does not provide a place in policy form-

[1]Howard Lee McBain, *The Living Constitution.* (New York: The Macmillan Company, 1928) 137.

[2]*Annual Report,* American Historical Association, 1901, Vol. I, p. 333, 336.

ulation for all of the parties at interest. One party machine rules while the opposition elements stand aside and hope for mistakes that will oust those in power. A presidential system operates in no such clear-cut fashion.

The chief executive is forced to seek middle ground. He cannot depend on his own party following. His measures are often supported by minority party members. The separation of executive and legislative branches gives both Congress and the president an opportunity to appeal to the voters. Stalemate is a constant possibility but in practice this has not brought serious consequences. In fact, Taft saw a positive value in the stalemate that may arise between Congress and the president after the mid-term election. "A system," he thought, "in which we may have an enforced rest from legislation for two years is not bad. It affords an opportunity for proper digestion of recent legislation and for the detection of its defects."[3] The separation between Congress and the White House is, in fact, an essential part in the successful operation of our system. With a powerful executive elected for a fixed period we must have some way of testing the voters' opinions. This our biennial Congressional elections provide. The tendency of mid-term Congressional elections to forecast the presidential elections following two years later is highly impressive.

In 1874 the Democrats carried the House; in 1876 Tilden obtained a popular majority although his Republican opponent managed to get the presidency. In 1878 the Democrats again won the Congressional elections, and two years later Garfield won a popular majority by the very narrow margin of only 915 votes. In both cases the evidence of a cyclical

[3]Reprinted from Taft: *Our Chief Magistrate and His Powers*, p. 12, by permission of Columbia University Press.

swing is clear even though a Republican president actually entered the White House. In 1882 the Republicans lost the House and in 1884 the presidency. In 1886 Democratic strength fell off and Cleveland was defeated two years later. In 1890 the House went strongly Democratic, and Cleveland returned to office in 1892. In 1894 the Republicans captured the House, and McKinley won in 1896. The G.O.P. held the House in the elections of 1898, 1902, and 1906, and gained the presidency in 1900, 1904, and 1908. The Democrats came into control of the House in 1910; Wilson was elected in 1912. The story was repeated in 1914 and 1916. The Republicans were back again in the House in 1918 and Harding was elected in 1920. The victories of Coolidge in 1924 and Hoover in 1928 were preceded by Republican House majorities in 1922 and 1926. The Democrats' return to power in 1930 forecast the election of 1932.

This persistent pattern is not offered as a device for predicting the future but rather as an explanation of the way in which our system tends to relieve the dissatisfactions that accumulate about the group in political control. The friction arising from the separation of powers cannot be explained away by failures in leadership or in adjustment between the legislature and executive. It is rather due to changes in the political base of Congress. The revolt that has so persistently occurred after the mid-term Congressional elections cannot be dismissed as caprice on the part of a disgruntled Congress. The electorate has had a chance to react to the early activities of the administration, and this reaction is expressed in Congress. Our presidents are given office for a fixed time and they can hold their position despite the grievances that may arise in the course of their term. This inevitably produces "cramps" in social and political relations. Congressional elections give early indication of such stresses. A presidential election serves in much greater measure to bring the control of the whole governmental apparatus in line with the change that has occurred over the country. It has often been said that the electorate tends rather to vote against an administration that has been in power than in favor of a new and untried candidate. This interpretation is strongly supported by the tendency of voters to indicate their party support two years before they know who the presidential candidate will be.

Our politicians, sensing the drift of opinion, must ask: Who is the candidate most likely to appeal to a majority of the electorate? They are prohibited from asking this question frankly when their party is committed to renominating a strong party leader such as William Jennings Bryan, or a presidential incumbent such as Cleveland, Grant, or Franklin D. Roosevelt. Under a parliamentary government party leaders have even less choice. The party leader will be prime minister not because he is most likely to appeal to the populace but because he controls the organization.

The presidents who come into office determined to put through a definite party program sooner or later discover their limitations. Those who act rather as symbols of national unity and as moderators of group interests maintain their power longer. As Pringle writes, Theodore Roosevelt "would progress to a certain point in his program to ward off socialism and unrest, and then make energetic efforts to appease the right wing."[4] This is the strategy innate in our system. Woodrow Wilson apparently never reconciled him-

[4] Henry F. Pringle, *Theodore Roosevelt*. (New York: Harcourt, Brace and Company, 1931) 427.

self to these limitations. War conditions helped him greatly in playing the role of prime minister.[5] He actually talked of resigning in the event that Congress overruled certain of his cherished measures.

Presidential responsibility is of great importance in considering administrative problems, but from the political point of view how far is it wise to go in the concentration of authority? If we make the stakes so high, we run the chance of disrupting the game of politics. Certain powerful interests may conclude that they cannot afford to lose the presidency! We have had in wartime an indication of the enormous centralization of power that is legally possible under our chief executive. But the temporary nature of this arrangement has always been assumed. As already stated, the president's control of Congress is based on influence rather than on authority. It is a contingent relationship. When it seems unlikely that the president will continue in office another term, his power begins to wane.

The possibility that a president can and may seek a third term is highly useful. It would be unwise to limit presidential tenure by law to two terms. This would in effect cut into the chief executive's second term since he could not maintain his influence to the end. The certainty of his political demise would encourage a desertion of supporters long before the fatal day.

Thus Pringle wrote of Theodore Roosevelt:

The President was no longer the potent influence he had been, for the simple reason that he would go out of office on March 5, 1909; it had been a mistake to announce in 1904 that he would never again be a Candidate for a Presidential nomination.[6]

[5]Binkley, op. cit., p. 228.
[6]Pringle, op. cit., p. 476.

So long as the chief executive can look forward to another term, congressmen see a possibility of receiving some reward for loyalty to the White House; but a president embarking upon a third term can expect trouble at least half way through this last term. This is one very strong objection to prolonging presidential terms. On the other hand, there may be instances when the need for continuity of policy is so great that a third term is justified.

In times of emergency, for example, the voter must decide whether a continuance in power of the existing administration is called for or whether the situation demands new leaders for a new task. It can be argued that continuity in policy is of tremendous importance when basic changes in the relations between industry and government are under way. One means of maintaining a consistent line of development is to be found in the maintenance of the same personnel, particularly at the higher levels. Gladstone exercised a persistent influence in Great Britain for over thirty years. His leadership coincides with a crucial period of empire development, and the imprint that he left on British administration is of enormous importance. In its effort to meet the demands made upon it by current economic problems, can the federal government be protected from marked shifts in policy?

Our system provides little opportunity for any one statesman to exercise an influence comparable to that of Gladstone. Our closest parallel may be found in the senatorial oligarchies that were so powerful in Congress around the turn of the century. The New Dealers apparently are similarly ambitious to protract their influence. Without regard to the merits of contending political forces, one effect of a long-sustained emergency will be so to entrench governmental control over industry as to alter permanently the face of our economy. The period of effective control in the last war was very brief. Not until the spring of 1918, about six months before the Armistice, was a reasonably effective control mechanism completed. Today the country has scarcely had time to react from the depression and the governmental activity resulting, before an even heavier burden has been imposed by foreign affairs. Under such circumstances the people will continue to look to the White House rather than to Congress for leadership. Our government provides for an alternation of presidential and Congressional power. At times when authority and action are needed, the chief executive can be given scope; but at two-year intervals, when Congressional elections occur, the voters have the opportunity to judge his course. There is danger in this, to be sure, but we cannot preordain the success of popular government. We can, however, seek to improve the mechanics of legislative-executive relations so that if and when Congress impedes the president we may feel confident that this is in response to the will of the voters and not due to a lack of knowledge or to political trickery within Congress.

To generalize about a relationship so dynamic as that between Congress and the chief executive is dangerous. Congress is no fixed entity—it is a group of human beings reshuffled at regular intervals by popular elections and shifted daily, even hourly, as different issues evoke varying reactions in the minds of individual members. The presidency is an office so colored by the personality of the incumbent and so affected by the current of the times that beyond the formal legal attributes of the position tremendous scope for self-expression remains. So in dealing with the president and Congress we face concomitant variables.

One of the most significant aspects of the relationships between the president and Congress is the ebb and flow of executive power. The increase in presidential authority comes as the result of popular demand for rapid and positive action. Powers are granted for temporary periods.

The need for fluidity in political relations can never safely be disregarded in the study of political institutions. There is no one best system. What is best suited for one set of conditions is ill adapted to others. To an extraordinary degree the relations between the chief executive and Congress are not spelled out in legal terms. Thus they become what the times and participants make them. Certain conditions clearly call for great power and initiative on the part of the president. Were his formal powers permanently increased to meet more easily the demands in times of crisis, would the nation rest content with such a concentration of authority in times of quietude? The answer may be made that the federal government has become committed to burdens of administration that call for positive leadership. There can be no doubt that the presidential office offers the only point for unified leadership. On the other hand, the whole concept of leadership in such terms is still tentative. Unless a rigid hierarchy is established and disciplined by adequate sanctions, leadership is not so much a matter of authority stretching downward as of loyalty extending upward. Even the general of an army, with all his means for control, is strongest when support is freely offered by each soldier, and the analogy is well applied to democratic government. Leadership is the obverse side of "followship" and fellowship. Hence the proposed strengthening of the presidential powers must be considered in relation to the circumstances which can make or break those powers.

In judging the adequacy of our institutions we are too inclined to look at the top and to ignore the substructure. Hopeful, some would make sweeping changes in the relations of Congress and the executive. Of greater intrinsic potentiality than such drastic and unpredictable changes are the minor changes that can be made further down, and that in their accumulated effect will preserve the structure and make it more effective at higher levels. This means multiplying the opportunities for each individual to contribute his own special skills and energies. These opportunities, however, cannot be written in terms of vague public spirit and the hollow hortatory ring of citizenship in the abstract, but of citizenship in terms of individual capacity and experience. In a society so constructed, the "checks and balances" at the top would have little use or meaning save as hypothetical safeguards against hypothetical abuses.

The fabric of democratic government can be pictured as composed of many strands. The strength of the fabric depends on the way in which these strands are interwoven. The integrity of these strands is best preserved not through isolation but through the skill with which they are related to the others: through the strength of the fabric as a whole the strength of each strand is maintained. As these threads are interwoven, different patterns emerge. In the intricacy and variety of these designs lies evidence of the imagination and vitality at work in our democratic society. Like the weavers of an Oriental carpet we sit close to our task, facing the seamy side of our designs and fingering the knots that make up the pattern.

But lack of perspective must not be allowed to detract

from appreciation of the product. A broad view of the last few decades discloses a most impressive record of relatively peaceful political adjustment to great economic changes within the United States. Much of this adjustment has been piecemeal and unplanned, but advances have been made on a broad basis of consent.

In the broadest social terms our political institutions have proved well adapted to the kind of life that this country knew during the nineteenth century, when allowing freedom for economic growth seemed sufficient.

But what of the present and of the future? Government is expected to make the economy function successfully. A formal structure established by a group of men whose great concern was with limiting the scope of state activity is now being utilized for constructive assistance in many areas of economic life. Here are real needs that must be faced. Even though we are still a continent geographically and politically, we have come of age economically as a nation. Our economy in becoming national requires governmental treatment in national terms.

These economic problems pose the question of how to apply our great resources to our great needs through channels of control based on the democratic ideas we cherish. Perhaps this is a traitorous question in that it suggests that we must find a way to eat our cake and have it too. It may seem obvious that a democracy which is based on the toleration of conflicting wills cannot be reconciled with planned controls of production and distribution, for social control must be predicated on unity and discipline. Nevertheless a tremendous middle ground for action remains between the logical extremes of individual freedom and a planned society. It is within this great area that we must work out our salvation. Our chances for success are better than those of any other nation professing democratic ideas: we have the economic margin which is indispensable to tolerance and good will.

In constructing our Constitution the Founding Fathers built on the assumption that man is prone to abuse power. They drew their magic circles of separate areas of government and set up strong taboos against infringement. Under this institutional grant of power diverse economic systems have developed with monopolists, small shopkeepers, independent farmers, share croppers, trade-unionists and the unemployed jostling together and trying to argue their diverse ways into workable compromises. Tremendous racial variety, rapid industrial expansion, sporadic religious and intellectual ferment: in the face of this pluralism what assumptions of man and his objectives could be safely taken as the basis for an integrated political life?

By limiting the sphere of government, by incorporating within the Constitution itself fundamental safeguards to individual freedom and by centering in no single institution final authority, our political machinery has maintained an extraordinary amount of flexibility.

For everyday purposes the uncertain balance of power between the executive and the legislature has been of crucial significance. If the economic answers were clear and men were agreed in their objectives, we might with more confidence attempt to express through our governmental institutions unified power and direction. In the world as we find it there is much to be said for a separation of powers which offers alternatives to a society uncertain of its direction but preferring to make its own mistakes rather than relinquish this privilege to any single gang of rulers.

In our American striving for efficiency and our tendency to favor direct action, we have at times been impatient with the conservatism of legal institutions. Yet so great is the strength of tradition or inertia that usually some way to achieve the desired goal had to be found short of tampering with constitutional or other long-established legal forms. The cry of dictatorship raised against Franklin D. Roosevelt's "court-packing" plan was doubtless prompted by partisanship, and yet the widespread revulsion was based on a habit of mind deeply ingrained. This profound and even emotional conviction that the courts must not be interfered with is a factor of the utmost importance in the continuity of constitutional government. Legal conservatism says "Stop!—let political inventiveness look elsewhere for ways and means." This puts a strain on ingenuity, but it removes the pressure from deeply rooted institutions. Efficiency and action are important; but so is the continuity and stability of governmental institutions.

The extent to which a particular *modus operandi* should be institutionalized is a matter for debate. Our Anglo-Saxon tradition tends to encourage an evolutionary approach. The governmental institutions that have demonstrated the greatest lasting powers have not been those consciously established or syllogistically arranged.

In all the talk of separation of powers there is a great deal of artificiality. In actual practice there must be a combination of the functions of legislating, executing, or adjudicating which in formal theory are supposed to be kept distinct. In practice we have achieved this in sufficient degree to weather an economic storm of awful magnitude and to face a world at war.

Why is it that the capacity of our system for action is so

often underestimated? One answer partially lies in the openness of our political squabbles. To the outsider, and even to ourselves, it is indeed a wonder that out of so much loud talking and petty maneuvering decisions are made and plans formulated. The matters that are quietly settled in parliamentary governments through discussion in cabinet meetings or in private party conferences are paraded and debated in public here. Our political leaders shout from one section of the country to another, from one end of Pennsylvania Avenue to the other, and from the Senate to the House. If we had well-articulated national party organizations, sternly disciplined, if we had a national ministry formally and actually dealing with public policy, if we had both legislative chambers held firmly in hand by this ministry, we could proceed with greater decorum. Observers accustomed to more orderly methods would then feel less dubious about the ability of our institutions to meet the demands of the present day.

In actual practice our system can respond quickly to emergency conditions once the public is convinced of the need. Presidential leadership sustained by a united people has power for any crisis.

In a time of divided purposes Congress can so obstruct action that no president can have his will; but when the goal is clear the branches of government can move as one.

Our governmental structure does not condemn us to inaction and delay; we are able to transcend the institutional devices that provide for checks and balances and deliberation. In emergency we are free to improvise but it does not follow from this that action and control are always to be given priority over deliberation and compromise.

Out of the infinite complexity of societal life, what phases are to be selected and built up into political institutions?

In our political institutions we have built on the assumption that concentrated power is dangerous in normal times. We have expressed our suspicion of strong leadership by hedging official position with various legal checks; but effective controls in time of emergency can be instituted with great rapidity. Once the general public realizes the need for united support behind the administration, the gap between Congress and the president is quickly closed. The concentration of authority is essential but its concentration in the wrong person is disastrous. This may be one consequence of a parliamentary system. It is a danger under our method of electing a president for a fixed term; but we have the great advantage of freshly surveying a wide field for selection. British leaders must serve a long apprenticeship to their parties. The fluidity of our system is a great safeguard.

The British system calls for strongly organized national parties. The small clique at the top could not be shaken loose. As one correspondent writes: "There are in Britain enough good brains—in business, in minor civil jobs, in the ranks of back-benchers on all sides of the House of Commons —to deal with problems even as great as those of today. But they were not utilized; they were allowed to plod along on jobs of comparative unimportance while the chief whip of the Conservative party machine and the old friends of Stanley Baldwin and Neville Chamberlain filled the important jobs."[7]

Our major parties are far too weak to enforce such control. We have no national bosses comparable to British party leaders.

Our system has certain other definite advantages that it

[7] *The New York Times Magazine,* June 30, 1940, p. 3.

is well to bear in mind. Periodic elections and overlapping terms of office provide stability that guards us from the brittleness of the French system. France has had twenty-one premiers since the World War. To hold power the premier was dependent upon the uncertain temper of the Chamber of Deputies. Our independent executive is not menaced by sheer political bickering. At the same time Congressional biennial election periods quickly bring discontents out into the open. The separation of power between Congress and president makes stalemate the constant threat of disagreement. Hence there is a persistent impetus to find some workable compromise. Parliamentary governments can more readily isolate criticism in the opposition party ranks and thus render them innocuous until a general election brings a new party machine to power.

Our system is highly sensitive to the opinion of voters. Our representatives must live or die politically on their capacity to satisfy their locality. As in no other country the success of the government rests boldly upon the capacity of individuals to manage their political affairs.

There is nothing inevitable about democracy. Whether our experience in self-government becomes an interlude in history or a way of life for future generations will be determined in our lifetimes. History has demonstrated again and again that rule falls to those who can most effectively consolidate and centralize power. Force has been the customary method: through dictatorship within and externally through military conquest.

To compete in such a world we must have effective government. The alternative is paralysis and chaos.

On the other hand, there is nothing inevitable about dictatorship. Tyrants did not arise in Europe until parliamentary government failed, torn asunder by factionalism and class conflict. Such dissensions weakened France long before Hitler struck. Our presidential system cannot function unless based on common underlying loyalties that induce unity up to the top. The integration must work throughout. It cannot be left to one man—the symbol—in the White House to "save the nation" or to "make democracy work." As Lynd writes: "Authority is a continuous two-way process, or it is tyranny. Our emphasis upon individualism has made us careless of the inescapable need in a democracy to organize responsibility and authority horizontally at the local base, and vertically up to the apex."[8]

In periods of crisis we find intensified both the need for authority and the dangers arising from conflicting purposes. In a democratic society there is agreement on fundamental values. Men accept the same symbols and respond to the same ideals. Ideological unity exists to which men express loyalty, but underlying are conflicts of interests that hold individuals in competing groups. To reconcile our differences we support political institutions which prescribe a procedure for peaceful adjustment. The presidential office is one such institution. The man in the White House is to guide the nation toward its common purpose. To the framers of the Constitution the chief magistrate was to be a moderator, not a crusader. Time and events have built the presidential office into a foremost position for national leadership. Yet the leader, to be effective, in a democratic society must remain a moderator at least in part. Today the president's means for control are stronger, but the stakes are higher also, and hence problems of adjustment are sharper.

[8]Robert S. Lynd, *Knowledge—For What?* (Princeton: Princeton University Press, 1939) 211–12.

The kind of man occupying the White House will profoundly affect the shape of things to come. Will he appeal to the voters with promises and arguments that will prepare them for dealing with future problems? Or will the symbols he uses be unrelated to the tasks ahead? For example, in a world largely dominated by Fascist powers, can democratic government hope to preserve both its own institutions and a private system of free business enterprise? Those who want the maximum of free enterprise must face the fact that this is really antithetical to wartime controls. The most practical point of view is to support a political system that will tolerate some degree of free enterprise while recognizing frankly that its ambit is inescapably restricted by the world in which we find ourselves. To demand free enterprise in a world of autarchy is to emulate the king who commanded the mounting tide to recede. From such extremism the tidal wave of war economics forces a retreat in order to escape the inevitable flood of events. On the other hand, we are not likely to fall into the same error of those Europeans who were ready to embrace Fascism as a way to preserve capitalism! More in keeping with American habits is our tendency to improvise the machinery for controls demanded by the crisis and freely grant the powers needed to preserve our democratic institutions. But lest these controls kill the very values they are expected to safeguard, power must ever remain contingent upon popular support. This accountability is implicit in the separation of power between Congress and the chief executive. Presidential leadership cannot be effective without continued Congressional support. This balance of powers can be a weakness only if we falter in our sense of national purpose.

If our democracy fails to meet the demands of the hour,

the fault will lie not with the system but with ourselves. In the ultimate reckoning the governance of a free people is an affair not of forms but of men.

Presidential leadership is the answer, but the successful leader under any system is he who fires a common loyalty within the souls of divergent individuals. Our democracy must stand upon our capacity to respond to a common cause.

APPENDIX I

War Powers of the President
The Code of Laws of the United States of America

Title 50—*WAR*

Chapter 1—COUNCIL OF NATIONAL DEFENSE

SECTION 1. *Creation, purpose, and composition of council.* A Council of National Defense is hereby established, for the coordination of industries and resources for the national security and welfare, to consist of the Secretary of War, the Secretary of the Navy, the Secretary of the Interior, the Secretary of Agriculture, the Secretary of Commerce, and the Secretary of Labor. (Aug. 29, 1916, c. 418, § 2, 39 Stat. 649.)

SECTION 2. *Advisory commission.* The Council of National Defense shall nominate to the President, and the President shall appoint, an advisory commission, consisting of not more than seven persons, each of whom shall have special knowledge of some industry, public utility, or the development of some natural resource, or be otherwise specially qualified, in the opinion of the council, for the performance of the duties hereinafter provided. The members of the advisory commission shall serve without compensation, but shall be allowed actual expenses of travel and subsistence when attending meetings of the commission or en-

147

gaged in investigations pertaining to its activities. The advisory commission shall hold such meetings as shall be called by the council or be provided by the rules and regulations adopted by the council for the conduct of its work. (Aug. 29, 1916, c. 418, § 2, 39 Stat. 649.)

SECTION 3. *Duties of council.* It shall be the duty of the Council of National Defense to supervise and direct investigations and make recommendations to the President and the heads of executive departments as to the location of railroads with reference to the frontier of the United States so as to render possible expeditious concentration of troops and supplies to points of defense; the coordination of military, industrial, and commercial purposes in the location of branch lines of railroad; the utilization of waterways; the mobilization of military and naval resources for defense; the increase of domestic production of articles and materials essential to the support of armies and of the people during the interruption of foreign commerce; the development of seagoing transportation; data as to amounts, location, method and means of production, and availability of military supplies; the giving of information to producers and manufacturers as to the class of supplies needed by the military and other services of the Government, the requirements relating thereto, and the creation of relations which will render possible in time of need the immediate concentration and utilization of the resources of the Nation. (Aug. 29, 1916, c. 418, § 2, 39 Stat. 649; Nov. 9, 1921, c. 119, § 3, 42 Stat. 212.)

SECTION 4. *Rules and regulations; subordinate bodies and committees.* The Council of National Defense shall adopt rules and regulations for the conduct of its work, which rules and regulations shall be subject to the approval of the President, and shall provide for the work of the advisory commission to the end that the special knowledge of such commission may be developed by suitable investigation, research, and inquiry and made available in conference and report for the use of the council; and the council may organize subordinate bodies for its assistance in special investigations, either by the employment of experts or by the creation of committees of specially qualified persons to serve without compensation, but to direct the investigations of experts so employed. (Aug. 29, 1916, c. 418, §2, 39 Stat. 650.)

SECTION 5. *Reports of activities and expenditures.* Reports shall be submitted by all subordinate bodies and by the advisory commission to the council, and from time to time the council shall report to the President or to the heads of executive departments upon special inquiries or subjects appropriate thereto, and an annual report to the Congress shall be submitted through the President, including as full a statement of the activities of the council and the agencies subordinate to it as is consistent with the public interest, including an itemized account of the expenditures made by the council or authorized by it, in as full detail as the public interest will permit: *Provided, however,* That when deemed proper the President may authorize, in amounts stipulated by him, unvouchered expenditures and report the gross sums so authorized not itemized. (Aug. 29, 1916, c. 418, § 2, 39 Stat. 650.)

Chapter 4—E S P I O N A G E

SECTION 36. [Relative to areas concerning which the disclosure of information is unlawful.] *Designation of prohibited places by proclamation.* The President in time of war or in case of national emergency may by proclamation designate any place other than those set forth in subsection (a) of section 31 of this title in which anything for the use of the Army or Navy is being prepared or constructed or stored as a prohibited place for the purpose of this chapter: *Provided,* That he shall determine that information with respect thereto would be prejudicial to the national defense. (June 15, 1917, c. 30, Title I, § 6, 40 Stat. 219.)

Chapter 5—ARSENAL, ARMORIES, ARMS, AND WAR MATERIAL GENERALLY

SECTION 78. *Gauges, dies, and tools for manufacture of arms.* The Secretary of War is authorized to prepare or cause to be prepared, to purchase or otherwise procure, such gauges, dies, jigs, tools, fixtures, and other special aids and appliances, including specifications and detailed drawings, as may be necessary for the immediate manufacture, by the Government and by private manufacturers, of arms, ammunition, and special equipment necessary to arm and equip the land forces likely to be required by the United States in time of war: *Provided,* That in the expenditure of any sums appropriated to carry out the purposes of this section the laws prescribing competition in the procurement of supplies by purchase shall not govern, whenever in the opinion of the Secretary of War such action will be for the best interest of the public service. (June 3, 1916, c. 134, § 123, 39 Stat. 215.)

SECTION 79. *Nitrate plants.* The President of the United States is authorized and empowered to make, or cause to be made, such investigation as in his judgment is necessary to determine the best, cheapest, and most available means for the production of nitrates and other products for munitions of war and useful in the manufacture of fertilizers and other useful products by water power or any other power as in his judgment is the best and cheapest to use; and is also authorized and empowered to designate for the exclusive use of the United States, if in his judgment such means is best and cheapest, such site or sites, upon any navigable or nonnavigable river or rivers or upon the public lands, as in his opinion will be necessary for carrying out the purposes of this section; and is further authorized to construct, maintain, and operate, at or on any site or sites so designated, dams, locks, improvement to navigation, power houses, and other plants and equipment or other means than water power as in his judgment is the best and cheapest, necessary or convenient for the generation of electrical or other power and for the production of nitrates or other products needed for munitions of war and useful in the manufacture of fertilizers and other useful products.

The President is authorized to lease, purchase, or acquire, by condemnation, gift, grant, or device such lands and rights of way as may be necessary for the construction and operation of such plants, and to take from any lands of the United States, or to purchase or acquire by condemnation materials, minerals, and processes, patented or otherwise, necessary for the construction and operation of such plants and for the manufacture of such products.

The products of such plants shall be used by the President for military and naval purposes to the extent that he may deem necessary, and any surplus which he shall determine is not required shall be sold and disposed of by him under such regulations as he may prescribe.

The President is authorized and empowered to employ such officers, agents, or agencies as may in his discretion be necessary to enable him to carry out the purposes herein specified, and to authorize and require such officers, agents, or agencies to perform any and all of the duties imposed upon him by the provisions hereof.

The plant or plants provided for under this section shall be constructed and operated solely by the Government and not in conjunction with any other industry or enterprise carried on by private capital. (June 3, 1916, c. 134, § 124, 39 Stat. 215.)

SECTION 80. *Procurement of war material; mobilization of industries.* The President, in time of war or when war is imminent, is empowered, through the head of any department of the Government, in addition to the present authorized methods of purchase or procurement, to place an order with any individual, firm, association, company, corporation, or organized manufacturing industry for such product or material as may be required, and which is of the nature and kind usually produced or capable of being produced by such individual, firm, company, association, corporation, or organized manufacturing industry.

Compliance with all such orders for products or material shall be obligatory on any individual, firm, association, company, corporation, or organized manufacturing industry or the responsible head or heads thereof and shall take precedence over all other orders and contracts theretofore placed with such individual, firm, association, company, corporation, or organized manufacturing industry, and any individual, firm, association, company, corporation, or organized manufacturing industry or the responsible head or heads thereof owning or operating any plant equipped for the manufacture of arms or ammunition, or parts of ammunition, or any necessary supplies or equipment for the Army, and any individual, firm, association, company, corporation, or organized manufacturing industry or the responsible head or heads thereof owning or operating any manufacturing plant, which, in the opinion of the Secretary of War shall be capable of being readily transformed into a plant for the manufacture of arms or ammunition, or parts thereof, or other necessary supplies or equipment, who shall refuse to give to the United States such preference in the matter of the execution of orders, or who shall refuse to manufacture the kind, quantity, or quality of arms or ammunition, or the parts thereof, or any necessary supplies or equipment, as ordered by the Secretary of War, or who shall refuse to furnish such arms, ammunitions, or parts of ammunition, or other supplies or equipment, at a reasonable price as determined by the Secretary of War, then, and in either such case, the President, through the head of any department of the Government, in addition to the present authorized methods of purchase or procurement herein provided for, is authorized to take immediate possession of any such plant or plants, and through the Ordnance Department of the United States Army, to manufacture therein in time of war or when war shall be imminent, such product or material as may be required, and any individual firm, company, association, or corporation, or organized manufacturing industry, or the responsible head or heads thereof, failing to comply with the provisions of this section shall be deemed guilty of a felony, and upon conviction shall be punished by imprisonment for not more than three years and by a fine not exceeding $50,000.

The compensation to be paid to any individual, firm, company, association, corporation, or organized manufacturing industry for its product or material, or as rental for use of any manufacturing plant while used by the United States, shall be fair and just.

The Secretary of War shall also make, or cause to be made, a complete list of all privately owned plants in the United States equipped to manufacture arms or ammunition, or the component parts thereof. He shall obtain full and complete information regarding the kind of arms or ammunition, or the component parts thereof, manufactured or that can be manufactured by each such plant, the equipment in each plant and the maximum capacity thereof. He shall also prepare, or cause to be prepared, a list of privately owned manufacturing plants in the United States capable of being readily transformed into ammunition factories, where the capacity of the plant is sufficient to warrant transforming such plant or plants into ammunition factories in time of war or when war shall be imminent; and as to all such plants the Secretary of War shall obtain full and complete information as to the equipment of each such plant, and he shall prepare comprehensive plans for transforming each such plant into an ammunition factory, or a factory in which to manufacture such parts of ammunition as in the opinion of the Secretary of War such plant is best adapted.

The President is authorized, in his discretion, to appoint a Board on Mobilization of Industries Essential for Military Preparedness, nonpartisan in character, and to take all necessary steps to provide for such clerical assistance as he may deem necessary to organize and coordinate the work hereinbefore described. (June 3, 1916, c. 134, § 120, 39 Stat. 213, 214.)

SECTION 82. *Procurement of ships and material during war;*

changes in contracts; commandeering factories, etc. (a) The word "person" as used in paragraphs (b), (c), next hereafter shall include any individual, trustee, firm, association, company, or corporation. The word "ship" shall include any boat, vessel, submarine, or any form of aircraft, and the parts thereof. The words "war material" shall include arms, armament, ammunition, stores, supplies, and equipment for ships and airplanes, and everything required for or in connection with the production thereof. The word "factory" shall include any factory, workshop, engine works, building used for manufacture, assembling, construction, or any process, and any shipyard or dockyard. The words "United States" shall include the Canal Zone and all territory and waters, continental and insular, subject to the jurisdiction of the United States.

(b) In time of war the President is hereby authorized and empowered, in addition to all other existing provisions of law:

First. Within the limits of the amounts appropriated therefor, to place an order with any person for such ships or war material as the necessities of the Government, to be determined by the President, may require and which are of the nature, kind, and quantity usually produced or capable of being produced by such person. Compliance with all such orders shall be obligatory on any person to whom such order is given, and such order shall take precedence over all other orders and contracts theretofore placed with such person. If any person owning, leasing, or operating any factory equipped for the building or production of ships or war material for the Navy shall refuse or fail to give to the United States such preference in the execution of such an order, or shall refuse to build, supply, furnish, or manufacture the kind, quantity, or quality of ships or war material so ordered at such reasonable price as shall be determined by the President, the President may take immediate possession of any factory of such person, or of any part thereof without taking possession of the entire factory, and may use the same at such times and in such manner as he may consider necessary or expedient.

Second. Within the limit of the amounts appropriated therefor, to modify or cancel any existing contract for the building, production, or purchase of ships or war material; and if any contractor shall refuse or fail to comply with the contract as so modified the President may take immediate possession of any factory of such contractor, or any part thereof without taking possession of the entire factory, and may use the same at such times and in such manner as he may consider necessary or expedient.

Third. To require the owner or occupier of any factory in which ships or war material are built or produced to place at the disposal of the United States the whole or any part of the output of such factory, and, within the limit of the amounts appropriated therefor, to deliver such output or parts thereof in such quantities and at such times as may be specified in the order at such reasonable price as shall be determined by the President.

Fourth. To requisition and take over for use or operation by the Government any factory, or any part thereof without taking possession of the entire factory, whether the United States has or has not any contract or agreement with the owner or occupier of such factory.

. . . .

(d) Whenever the United States shall cancel or modify any contract, make use of, assume, occupy, requisition, or take over any factory or part thereof, or any ships or war material, in accordance with the provisions of paragraph (b), it shall make just compensation therefor, to be determined by the President, and if the amount thereof so determined by the President is unsatisfactory to the person entitled to receive the same, such person shall be paid fifty per centum of the amount so determined by the President and shall be entitled to sue the United States to recover such further sum as added to said fifty per centum shall make up such amount as will be just compensation therefor, in the manner provided for by paragraph (20) of section 41 of

Title 28 and section 250 of Title 28. (Mar. 4, 1917, c. 180, 39 Stat. 1192.)

•   •   •   •   •   •   •

SECTION 91. *Educational orders for munitions of special or technical design: bids.* The Secretary of War is hereby authorized to place educational orders for munitions of war of special or technical design, or both, noncommercial in character (hereinafter called "special munitions"), and essential accessories and parts thereof needed in the military service, with commercial concerns to familiarize commercial and manufacturing establishments with the manufacture of such munitions and such accessories and parts. In arranging for placing such educational orders, bids shall be solicited only from such establishments as, in the Secretary's judgment, will be competent in time of war to manufacture the particular class of special munitions with respect to which the bid is solicited. In the determination of which classes of special munitions are to be manufactured under this subchapter, and in the determination of which of the solicited bidders is to be awarded any contract, the Secretary shall have regard solely to the selection of such classes of special munitions and of such bidders as will, in his judgment, under all the circumstances, best serve the interest of the United States and best promote the cause of national defense. The Secretary of War shall enter into no contract under this section without the approval of the President. (June 16, 1938, c. 458, § 1, Stat. 707.)

•   •   •   •   •   •   •

Chapter 11—ACQUISITION OF AND EXPENDITURES ON LAND FOR NATIONAL-DEFENSE PURPOSES

SECTION 171. *Methods of acquiring title; condemnation, purchase, and donation.* The Secretary of War may cause proceedings to be instituted in the name of the United States, in any court having jurisdiction of such proceedings for the acquirement by condemnation of any land, temporary use thereof or other interest therein, or right pertaining thereto, needed for the site, location, construction, or prosecution of works for fortifications, coast defenses, military training camps, and for the construction and operation of plants for the production of nitrate and other compounds and the manufacture of explosives and other munitions of war and for the development and transmission of power for the operations of such plants; such proceedings to be prosecuted in accordance with the laws relating to suits for the condemnation of property of the States wherein the proceedings may be instituted: *Provided,* That when the owner of such land, interest, or rights pertaining thereto shall fix a price for the same, which in the opinion of the Secretary of War shall be reasonable, he may purchase or enter into a contract for the use of the same at such price without further delay: *Provided further,* That the Secretary of War is authorized to accept on behalf of the United States donations of land and the interest and rights pertaining thereto required for the above-mentioned purposes: *And provided further,* That when such property is acquired in time of war, or the imminence thereof, upon the filing of the petition for the condemnation of any land, temporary use thereof or other interest therein or right pertaining thereto to be acquired for any of the purposes aforesaid, immediate possession thereof may be taken to the extent of the interest to be acquired and the lands may be occupied and used for military purposes. (Aug. 18, 1890,

c. 797, § 1, 26 Stat. 316; July 2, 1917, c. 35, 40 Stat. 241; Apr. 11, 1918, c. 51, 40 Stat. 518.)

SECTION 172. *Acquisition of property for production of lumber.* The provisions of section 171 of this title in all respects together with all its privileges and benefits are extended to the right of condemnation of standing or fallen timber, sawmills, camps, machinery, logging roads, rights-of-way, equipment, materials, supplies, and any works, property, or appliances suitable for the effectual production of such lumber and timber products, for the Army, Navy, United States Shipping Board, or the United States Shipping Board Merchant Fleet Corporation. The right to institute such condemnation proceedings is conferred upon the Secretary of War, the Secretary of the Navy, and the chairman of the United States Shipping Board and the United States Shipping Board Merchant Fleet Corporation, individually or collectively. Such right of condemnation shall be exercised by such officials only for the purpose of obtaining such property when needed for the production, manufacture, or building aircraft, dry docks, or vessels, their apparel or furniture, for housing of Government employees in connection with the Army, Navy, or the United States Shipping Board and the United States Shipping Board Merchant Fleet Corporation, and for the procurement of materials and equipment for aircraft, dry docks and vessels The jurisdiction of such condemnation proceedings is hereby vested in the district courts of the United States, where the property which is sought to be condemned or any part thereof is located or situated regardless of the value of the same.

And the President is authorized through any department or the United States Shipping Board or said Fleet Corporation to sell and dispose of any lands or interests in real estate acquired for the production of lumber and timber products, and to sell any logs, manufactured or partly manufactured or otherwise procured for the Army, Navy, or United States Shipping Board Merchant Fleet Corporation, or resulting from such manufacture or procurement, either to individuals, corporations, or foreign

States or governments, at such price as he shall determine acting through his above representatives selling or disposing of the same, and the proceeds of such sale shall be returned to the appropriations which bore the expense of such procurement. (July 9, 1918, c. 143, subchapter XV, § 8, 40 Stat. 888; Feb. 11, 1927, c. 104, § 1, 44 Stat. 1083.)

Title 10—*ARMY*

Chapter 31—TRANSPORTATION OF TROOPS AND SUPPLIES; ARMY TRANSPORT SERVICE

SECTION 1361. *Control of transportation systems in time of war.* The President, in time of war, is empowered, through the Secretary of War, to take possession and assume control of any system or systems of transportation, or any part thereof, and to utilize the same, to the exclusion as far as may be necessary of all other traffic thereon, for the transfer or transportation of troops, war material and equipment, or for such other purposes connected with the emergency as may be needful or desirable. (Aug. 29, 1916, c. 418, § 1, 39 Stat. 645.)

SECTION 1362. *Preference to shipments of troops, etc.* In time of war or threatened war preference and precedence shall, upon the demand of the President of the United States, be given over all other traffic, for the transportation of troops and material of war and carriers shall adopt every means within their control to facilitate and expedite the military traffic. And in time of peace shipments consigned to agents of the United States for its use shall be delivered by the carriers as promptly as possible and without regard to any embargo that may have been declared, and no such embargo shall apply to shipments so consigned. (Feb. 4, 1887, c. 104, § 6, 24 Stat. 380; Mar. 2, 1889, c. 382, § 1, 25 Stat. 855; June 29, 1906, c. 3591, § 2, 34 Stat. 586; Aug. 29, 1916, c. 417, 39 Stat. 604.)

Title 40—*PUBLIC BUILDINGS, PROPERTY, AND WORKS*

Chapter 5—HOURS OF LABOR ON PUBLIC WORKS

SECTION 276a. *Rate of wages for laborers and mechanics.* Every contract in excess of $5,000 in amount, to which the United States or the District of Columbia is a party, which requires or involves the employment of laborers or mechanics in the construction, alteration, and/or repair of any public buildings of the United States or the District of Columbia within the geographical limits of the States of the Union or the District of Columbia, shall contain a provision to the effect that the rate of wage for all laborers and mechanics employed by the contractor or any subcontractor on the public buildings covered by the contract shall be not less than the prevailing rate of wages for work of a similar nature in the city, town, village, or other civil division of the State in which the public buildings are located, or in the District of Columbia if the public buildings are located there, and a further provision that in case any dispute arises as to what are the prevailing rates of wages for work of a similar nature applicable to the contract which cannot be adjusted by the contracting officers, the matter shall be referred to the Secretary of Labor for determination and his decision thereon shall be conclusive on all parties to the contract: *Provided,* That in case of national emergency the President is authorized to suspend the provisions of this section. (Mar. 3, 1931, c. 411, § 1, 46 Stat. 1494.)

SECTION 326. *Suspension of eight-hour law in case of emergency; overtime pay.* In case of national emergency the President is authorized to suspend provisions of law prohibiting more than eight hours labor in any one day of persons engaged upon work covered by contracts with the United States: *Provided,* That the wages of persons employed upon such contracts shall be computed on a basic day rate of eight hours' work, with overtime rates to be paid for at not less than time and one-half for all hours work in excess of eight hours. (Mar. 4, 1917, c. 180, 39 Stat. 1192.)

Title 47—*TELEGRAPHS, TELEPHONES, AND RADIO TELEGRAPHS*

Chapter 5—WIRE OR RADIO COMMUNICATION

SECTION 606. *War powers of President.* (a) During the continuance of a war in which the United States is engaged, the President is authorized, if he finds it necessary for the national defense and security, to direct that such communications as in his judgment may be essential to the national defense and security shall have preference or priority with any carrier subject to this chapter. He may give these directions at and for such times as he may determine, and may modify, change, suspend, or annul them and for any such purpose he is hereby authorized to issue orders directly, or through such person or persons as he designates for the purpose, or through the Commission. Any carrier complying with any such order or direction for preference or priority herein authorized shall be exempt from any and all provisions in existing law imposing civil or criminal penalties, obligations, or liabilities upon carriers by reason of giving preference or priority in compliance with such order or direction.

(b) It shall be unlawful for any person during any war in which the United States is engaged to knowingly or willfully, by physical force or intimidation by threats of physical force, obstruct or retard or aid in obstructing or retarding interstate or foreign communication by radio or wire. The President is hereby authorized, whenever in his judgment the public interest requires, to employ the armed forces of the United States to prevent any such obstruction or retardation of communication: *Provided,* That nothing in this section shall be construed to repeal, modify, or affect either section 17 of Title 15 or section 52 of Title 29.

(c) Upon proclamation by the President that there exists war or a threat of war or a state of public peril or disaster or other national emergency, or in order to preserve the neutrality of the United States, the President may suspend or amend, for such time as he may see fit, the rules and regulations applicable to any or all stations within the jurisdiction of the United States as prescribed by the Commission, and may cause the closing of any station for radio communication and the removal therefrom of its apparatus and equipment, or he may authorize the use or control of any such station and/or its apparatus and equipment by any department of the Government under such regulations as he may prescribe, upon just compensation to the owners.

(d) The President shall ascertain the just compensation for such use or control and certify the amount ascertained to Congress for appropriation and payment to the person entitled thereto. If the amount so certified is unsatisfactory to the person entitled thereto, such person shall be paid only 75 per centum of the amount and shall be entitled to sue the United States to recover such further sum as added to such payment of 75 per centum will make such amount as will be just compensation for the use and control. Such suit shall be brought in the manner provided by paragraph 20 of section 41 of Title 28, or by section 250 of Title 28. (June 19, 1934, c. 652, § 606, 48 Stat. 1104.)

The president may also initiate important wartime measures under his power, within certain limits, to transfer, consolidate, or abolish governmental agencies for purposes of economy and efficiency (Public Resolution No. 19—76th Congress); under his power to suspend, for a period of not more than ninety days, all trading in registered securities on any national securities exchange (15 U.S.C. 78); under his power to vary the gold component of the dollar and put the United States on a bimetallic standard by decreeing unlimited coinage of silver (31 U.S.C. 821); and under his power to prescribe rules and regulations with respect to the possession, use, and importation or exportation of gold (12 U.S.C. 95). The Federal Power Commission, appointed by the president, may in wartime require such temporary connections of facilities, generation, and utilization of electrical power as in its judgment will best meet the emergency and serve the public interest (15 U.S.C. 824). Through the Maritime Commission the president may in case of emergency requisition any vessel documented under the laws of the United States (46 U.S.C. 1242); and he has the power to utilize stock piles accumulated by the procurement division of the Treasury on the joint order of the Secretary of War and the Secretary of the Navy, a power extending to June 30, 1943 (Public Resolution No. 117—76th Congress). The War, Navy, or Commerce departments may acquire lands capable of producing helium gas when that is necessary to meet the needs of the Army and Navy and other agencies of the federal government (50 U.S.C. 161–66).

APPENDIX II

Presidential Cabinets from Abraham Lincoln to Franklin D. Roosevelt

Abraham Lincoln (1861) through Franklin D. Roosevelt (April, 1940)—24 Administrations

Total of 308 cabinet posts filled (counting changes in secretaries and not individuals; i.e., one man may be counted two or more times).

Formerly members of the House:	18
Formerly members of the Senate:	8
Formerly members of both House and Senate:	8
Directly from House to Cabinet:	12

Reappointments to Cabinet again from this group:	4
Directly from Senate to Cabinet:	13
Reappointments to Cabinet again from this group:	6
Members of both House and Senate, appointed directly from Senate:	8
Reappointments to Cabinet again from this group:	4
No Congressional service:	227

Congressional background of cabinet members in each administration from Lincoln (1861) to Franklin D. Roosevelt (April, 1940)

	Per Cent		Per Cent
Lincoln—12 posts:		Grant—13 posts:	
4 S		2 R & S	
2 R	50	1 S	
		3 R	46
Lincoln—7 posts:		Grant—16 posts:	
1 S	14	2 R & S	
Johnson—13 posts:		2 S	
3 S	23	1 R	31

	Per Cent			Per Cent
Hayes—10 posts:		T. Roosevelt—20 posts:		
2 R & S		3 R		15
2 S		Taft—11 posts:		
3 R	70	—		—
Garfield—7 posts:		Wilson—13 posts:		
2 R & S		4 R		31
1 S	42	Wilson—16 posts:		
Arthur—17 posts:		5 R		31
2 R & S		Harding—13 posts:		
4 S	35	1 R & S		
Cleveland—11 posts:		2 S		
1 R & S		1 R		31
2 S	27	Coolidge—11 posts:		
Harrison—11 posts:		1 R & S		
2 R & S		1 S		18
3 R	45	Coolidge—14 posts:		
Cleveland—12 posts:		1 R & S		
1 R & S		2 S		21
2 R	25	Hoover—13 posts:		
McKinley—14 posts:		1 R		8
1 R & S		F. D. Roosevelt—12 posts:		
2 R	21	2 R & S		17
McKinley—9 posts:		F. D. Roosevelt—16 posts:		
1 R	11	2 R & S		13
T. Roosevelt—17 posts:				
4 R	24			

R & S—formerly member of House and Senate.
S—formerly member of Senate.
R—formerly member of House.

Geographical distribution of cabinet posts—Lincoln (1861) through Franklin D. Roosevelt (April 1, 1940)

Alabama—1	Kentucky—6
Arkansas—1	Louisiana—2
California—12	Maine—5
Colorado—5	Maryland—5
Connecticut—6	Massachusetts—22
Delaware—1	Michigan—6
District of Columbia—7	Minnesota—6
Georgia—2	Mississippi—1
Illinois—20	Missouri—14
Indiana—17	Nebraska—2
Iowa—20	New Hampshire—1
Kansas—3	New Jersey—6

New Mexico—1
New York—46
North Carolina—2
Ohio—23
Oklahoma—1
Oregon—2
Pennsylvania—26
South Carolina—2

Tennessee—7
Texas—5
Utah—2
Virginia—4
Vermont—2
Washington—1
West Virginia—3
Wisconsin—6

Geographical distribution of individual cabinet members— Lincoln (1861) through Franklin D. Roosevelt (April, 1940)

Alabama—1
Arkansas—1
California—6
Colorado—2
Connecticut—3
Delaware—1
District of Columbia—3
Georgia—2
Illinois—15
Indiana—9
Iowa—10
Kansas—2
Kentucky—3
Louisiana—1
Maine—3
Maryland—3
Massachusetts—15
Michigan—6
Minnesota—4
Mississippi—1
Missouri—10

Nebraska—2
New Hampshire—1
New Jersey—4
New Mexico—1
New York—29
North Carolina—1
Ohio—16
Oklahoma—1
Oregon—1
Pennsylvania—13
South Carolina—2
Tennessee—6
Texas—4
Utah—1
Virginia—2
Vermont—2
Washington—1
West Virginia—4
Wisconsin—5
Army—1

Index

Adams, Alva B., and budgetary procedure, 83

Adams, John, quoted, 6; and separation of powers, 119

Adams, Samuel Hopkins, *Incredible Era*, 105 n

Administration and Congress, importance of close relationship between, 115 ff.

Advisory Council on Social Security, 120, 121; *Final Report* (Dec. 10, 1938), 122 n

Akerson, George, 107

Aldrich, Nelson W., 51

American Historical Association, *Annual Report*, 1901, Vol. I., 129 n

American Legion, and universal draft, 17; and the Economy bill, 61

American Magazine, The (Aug. 1929), 72 n

American Mercury, The (Dec. 1929). 107 n

Arnold, Thurman, 85

Ashurst, Henry F., 39

Baker, Newton D., and presidential power, 16

Baker, R. S., 105 n

Balance of power, between executive and legislature, 139

Baldwin, Stanley, 142

Bankhead, John H., 120

Barkley, Alben W., quoted, 80

Baruch, B. M., *Taking the Profits Out of War*, 16 n

Beard, Charles A., 88

Binkley, W. E., *The Powers of the President: Problems of American Democracy*, 49 n

Black, Henry Campbell, quoted, 76; *The Relation of the Executive Power to Legislation*, 76 n

Blain, J. G., 97

"Blocs," 35, 42 ff.

Borah, W. E., 32, 100; clash with President Roosevelt and Cordell Hull on foreign affairs, 89–90

Brown, George Rothwell, quoted, 33; *The Leadership of Congress*, 33 n, 99 n

Brown, Walter F., 107

Browning, Gordon, and Economy bill, 59–60

Bryan, W. J., 99, 132

Bryce, James, on party leadership,

27; *The American Commonwealth,* 27 n

Budget Act of 1921, 82

Budget, Bureau of, 110; relations with Congressional committees, 81

Budget procedure, in House and Senate, 81

Budget review agency, proposed, 82

Buell, R. L., quoted, 87, 89; *Isolated America,* 87 n

Burke, James F., 107

Burleson, Albert S., 99

Burton, T. E., 100

Bushey, L. White, *Uncle Joe Cannon,* 51 n

Business interests, opposed to presidential leadership, 7

Byrd, Harry Flood, 85

Byrns, Joseph W., Jr., 57, 114

Cabinet members, advisability of permission to have seats in Congress, 92 ff.; compared to British practice, 95

Cameron, Simon, 97

Cannon, Joseph, relations with President Theodore Roosevelt, 50

Carpenter, Fred W., 103

Chamberlain, Sir Neville, 129, 142

Checks and Balances, 13; Whig principle of, 3–4

Chicago Tribune, and dictatorship, 17

Christian, G. B., Jr., 105

Closure rule, Senate and, 33

Cleveland, Grover, 47, 131, 132; cabinet appointees, 98; and tariff question, 125

Concentration of power, in the President, 15–16; United States, British and French systems contrasted, 142–43

Congress, and "special interests," 9;

President's formal powers relating to, 11; party control of, 27; lack of co-operation between both branches of, 27–28; as a representative assembly, 30; maintenance of discipline in, 33 ff.; proposals for change in relations between President and, Ch. IV, pp. 73–91; creation of legislative councils in, 80; relations to President, 136

Congressional behavior, Ch. II, pp. 21–45

Congressional-executive relations, 7–8

Conkling, Roscoe, 97

Connecticut, legislative council in, 79

Connery, Lawrence J., and Economy bill, 60

Coolidge, Calvin, quoted, 48, 68, 72, 131; and soldiers' bonus, 49; and World Court, 49; and Japanese exclusion, 49; "The President Lives under a Multitude of Eyes," *The American Magazine* (Aug. 1929), 72 n; cabinet appointees, 99–100

Cortelyou, George B., as secretary to President McKinley, and first Secretary of Commerce, 102

Couzens, James, 32

Davis, James J., on neutrality legislation, 88

Democracy, and tolerance, 18

Democratic Convention, 1940, and New Deal control, 25

Democratic government, structure of, 137 ff.

Democratic steering committee, 55 ff.

Dictatorship, 18–19; and presidential leadership, 71

Dieterich, William H., and holding company bill, 39
Dill, Clarence C., 66
"Discharge rule," 35–36
Division of Government Reports, 110
Doughton, Robert L., 31, 114
Dunn, A. W., 102; *From Harrison to Harding*, 103 *n*

Early, Stephen, 108
Economy act, 66
Economy bill, debate on, 59 ff.
Economy committee, creation of, 58
Elliott, W. Y., *The Need for Constitutional Reform*, 172 *n*
Expenditures, Congressional responsibility for, 77 ff
"Experts," questionable judgment of, 116–17

Farley, James A., and party organization, 75
Farm relief, movements toward, 120 ff.
Fascism, and increased executive power, 16
Filibustering, Senate and, 33
Fleming, D. F., *The Treaty Veto of the American Senate*, 86 *n*
Foreign affairs, relationship between Congress and President in regard to, 86
Foreign policy, proposed joint committee on, 89
Founding Fathers, views on choice of President, 3–5
Franklin, Ben, quoted, 20
Fuess, Claude, *Carl Schurz*, 97 *n*

Garfield, James N., 130, cabinet appointees, 97

Garner, J. N., quoted, 90; vote on Veterans' Compensation, 67
Gaus, John, quoted, 124; *Frontiers of Public Administration*, 124 *n*
Gladstone, W. E., 134
Goodnow, F. J., quoted, 114; *Politics and Administration*, 115 *n*
Governmental authority, distribution of, 14–15
Grant, President, 132; cabinet appointees, 97
Great Britain, conservative party in, 129; Prime Minister as director of national party machine, 74
Greenwood, Arthur H., and steering committee, 56

Hale, Eugene, 51
Harding, President, 48, 131
Harlan, Byron B., 94
Harper's Weekly (March 18, 1911), 103 *n*, 104 *n*
Harrison, Pat, 114
Harrison, President, 47
Hassett, William D., 108
Hatch Act, and federal job holders, 25
Hayes, President, cabinet appointees, 97
Hilles, Charles D., 104
Hinsdale, Mary, *A History of the President's Cabinet*, 97 *n*
Holding company, legislation, 38 ff.
Hoover, President, 131; relations with Congress, 52; and economic disruption, 125–26
Hoover, Irwin Hood, on presidential routine, 47–49; *Forty-Two Years in the White House*, 48 *n*; quoted, 103
Horner, Henry, 79
House, Col. E. H., 100

House of Commons, party voting in, 129

Hull, Cordell, on foreign affairs, 89–90

Illinois, legislative councils in, 78

Independent, The (Aug. 15, 1912), 105 *n;* and position of Secretary to President, 104

Independent commissions, value and responsibility of, 115 ff.

I.C.C., questionable functions of, 118

Jackson, President, his kitchen cabinet, 100

Johnson, General Hugh S., quoted, 43

Johnston, Olin D., 25

Joint Committee on Internal Revenue Taxation, functions of, 84

Joint Policy Committee, 91

Jones, Jesse, 101

Jones, Marvin, 120

Jones, Wesley L., 32

Judicial review, and presidential responsibility, 26

Kentucky, legislative council in, 79

King, William H., and proposed Congressional budget committee, 83

Kings, foundation of authority of, compared to the President, 4

La Follette Civil Liberties Committee, 85

Lamont, Daniel S., 105

Landis, James M., *The Administrative Process,* 116 *n;* and separation of powers, 116

Lane, F. K., 99

Laski, Harold, *The American Presidency,* 94 *n*

Legislative councils, in state governments, 77 ff.

Legislative council, proposals for Congress, 77–78

Liberal discharge rule, 34

Lincoln, President, denounced as dictator, 17; cabinet appointees, 96

Lipson, Leslie, *The American Governor from Figurehead to Leader,* 75 *n*

Lobbyists, and Congress, 21

Loeb, William, Jr., 102

Lonergan, Augustine, and holding company bill, 39

Long, H. C., 66

Lowell, A. L., "The Influence of Party upon Legislation," 129

Luce, Robert, quoted, 23, 29, 95; *Legislative Procedure,* 23 *n; Congress, An Explanation,* 95 *n*

Luetscher, George D., *Early Political Machinery,* 5 *n*

Lynd, R. S., quoted, 144; *Knowledge —For What?,* 144 *n*

McAdoo, William G., on Wilson's cabinet appointees, 98; *Crowded Years,* 99 *n*

McBain, Howard Lee, quoted, 128–29; *The Living Constitution,* 129 *n*

McDuffie, John, and the "discharge rule," 35

McKinley, President, 47, 101, 131

MacMahon, Arthur, quoted, 96

MacMahon and Millet, *Federal Administrators,* 96 *n*

Mellon, Andrew J., 100

Morgenthau, Secretary, on reform of budget procedure, 82

National defense, requirements for, 18

National economy, problems of, 138 ff.

National policy, presidential influence and control over, 21

National Resources Board, 110

National Resources Committee, 121

National unity, as symbolized in the presidency, 14

Neutrality Commission, 88

New Deal, the, leadership of, 24; and W.P.A. workers, 25; presidential policies of, 37

New Deal administration, first, 52 ff.

New Deal Congress, first, attitude toward its members, 33–34; democratic control of, 56 ff.

New Dealers, desire for long influence in national affairs, 134–35

New York Times, and creation of legislative council in Congress, 79–80

New York Times (July 13, 1939), 80 n

New York Times (Jan. 15, 1925), 106 n

New York Times (July 23, 1939), 108 n

New York Times Magazine, The, (July 30, 1940), 142 n

Newton, Walter H., 106

Norris, George W., 32

Norton, Charles D., 103

Nuisance tax bill, 113

O'Connor, John, and "discharge rule," 35

Outlook, The (June 11, 1910), 103 n

Old-age security. *See* Social Security

Party control, in Congress, 22–23; and first New Deal Congress, 56 ff.

Party government, and the President, 4–5; and strong executive, 5

Party leadership, 26–27

Party machines, control of, in Great Britain and U.S., compared, 74

Party organization, and control of Congress, 23–24; James A. Farley and, 75

Party system, and governmental structure, 25–26

Party voting, in Parliament and Congress compared, 129

Patronage, effectiveness of, as means of party control, 70; lack of in British system, 74 ff.

Political Science Quarterly (Oct.-Dec., 1937), 111 n

Porter, John A., 101

Pressure groups, 74

Presidency, as symbol of national unity, 128

President, dependence on Congress, 1; as politician and statesman, 1–2; as a factor in local politics, 2; and the electoral college, 3; Founding Fathers' conception of type and duties of, 3–5; foundation of authority, compared to kings, 4; merits and defects in early system of selection, 4–6; as "tribune of the people," 8; personal nature of office of, 10–11; formal powers relating to Congress, 11; as chief administrator and legislator, 12; methods of dealing with Congress contrasted, 47 ff.; proposed changes in relation to Congress, Ch. IV, pp. 73–91; his entourage, Ch. V, pp. 92–110; office of secretary to, 101 ff.; clerical staff, growth and functions of, 107–8; influence of mid-term

Congressional elections on choice of, 130 ff.; relations to Congress, 136; war powers of, Appendix I, pp. 147–63

Presidential cabinets, from Lincoln to F. D. Roosevelt, Appendix II, pp. 164–66

Presidential leadership, opposed by business interests, 7; necessity for, 14–15; strength of, Ch. VII, pp. 128–46; supreme task of, 18; effectiveness of, 20; and dictatorship, 71; essential qualities for, 71

Presidential control, methods of, Ch. III, pp. 46–72

Presidential power, in emergencies, 15–16; political basis of, Ch. I, pp. 1–20; and war, 16

Presidential responsibility, limits of, Ch. VI, pp. 111–27

Presidential secretary, beginnings and growth of office, 101 ff.

Presidential succession, 5

Presidential veto. *See* Veto

President's Committee on Administrative Management, recommendations and developments of, 109–10

President's Committee on Farm Tenancy, 120

Prime Minister, as supreme political power, 128

Pringle, H. F., quoted, 132, 133; *Theodore Roosevelt,* 132 n

Public policy, leadership in, 9

Putney, Bryant, "Participation by Congress in Control of Foreign Policy," *Editorial Research Reports* (Nov. 9, 1939)

Rainey, Henry T., 57; and the "discharge rule," 34; and Steering Committee, 55

Randall, James G., *Constitutional Problems under Lincoln,* 16 n, 17 n; quoted, 16

Rayburn, Sam, and the holding company bill, 41

Reconstruction Finance Corporation, 101

Regulatory commissions, 13

Richey, Lawrence, 107

Robinson, J. Will, 113

Rogers, Lindsay, quoted, 111; "The American Presidential System," *Political Science Quarterly* (Oct.-Dec., 1937), 111 n

Roosevelt, Franklin D., 11, 132; and St. Lawrence waterway, 9; and 1938 election, 25; and first New Deal administration, 52 ff.; relations to 73d Congress, 63 ff.; opposition to his economy program, 66 ff.; and radio appeal, 70; tax message, 112 ff.; "court packing," 140

Roosevelt, Theodore, 47, 102; relations with Speaker Cannon, 50; clashes with Congress, 51; *Theodore Roosevelt: An Autobiography,* 51 n; and third term, 133

Royal Commissions, success of in Sweden, 124

Rules Committee, functions of, 37

St. Lawrence waterway, 9

Sanders, Everett, 106

Sectional and group interests, 22

Selective veto. *See* Veto

Seniority rule, 30–31; and internal organization of Congress, 36 ff.

Separation of powers, 8, 16, 119–21, 139 ff.

Slemp, Bascom, 105

Smith, Harold D., on budget procedure, 81

Smoot, Reed, 32

Snell, Bertrand H., attitude toward New Deal administration, 54, 57

Social security, 121 ff.

Soldiers' bonus, 49

Special administrative agencies, and special interests, 117–18

Special commissions. *See* Independent commissions

"Special interests," and Congress, 9; and discharge rule, 35; and special administrative agencies, 117

State reorganization, results of, 75–76

Stearns, Frank, 100

Steering committee, 55 ff.

Story, Joseph, quoted, 46

Swedish Royal Commissions, success of, 124

Taft, President, 47, 94, 103; quoted, 130; *Our Chief Magistrate and His Powers*, 130 n

Temporary National Economic Committee, proposed continuance of, 85–86

Thompson, Carmi, 104

Third term, reasons for and against, 133–34

Thomas, Elmer, 89

Tilden, Samuel J., 130

Totalitarianism, and democracy, 18–19

Treaty ratification, and the Senate, 87

Tumulty, Joseph P., 105; *Woodrow Wilson as I Knew Him*, 105 n

Twentieth Amendment, 11

U.S. Information Service, 110

Vandenburg, Arthur H., 122

Veterans' expenditures, proposed curtailment in, 66

Veto power, 12

Veto, presidential, criticism of present method, 76–77

Volstead Act, modification of, 62

Wallace, Henry A., Chairman of Farm Tenancy Committee, 120

Walsh, Correa Moylan, *The Political Science of John Adams*, 6 n

War powers, of President, Appendix I, pp. 147–63

Washington, George, relations to Senate on discussion of treaty with Southern Indians, 86

Watson, Brigadier General E. M., 108

Watson, James E., on Hoover administration, 52; *As I Knew Them*, 52 n

Wheeler, Burton K., and holding company bill, 39

Whig concept of separation of powers, 8

White, W. A., on Bascom Slemp, as secretary to President Coolidge, 105–6; *A Puritan in Babylon*, 106 n

Wilson, W. B., 99

Wilson, Woodrow, 11, 47, 131, 132; *Constitutional Government in the United States*, 11 n; messages to Congress, 49; clashes with Congress, 51; and Peace Conference, 87; cabinet appointees, 98; and world reorganization, 125

Wisconsin, legislative council in, 77–78

Woodrum, Clifton A., 58

World's Work, The (Dec. 1924), 100 n

Printed in the United States
137397LV00008B/6/P